# PRAISE FOR *THE OTHER SIDE OF GRIEF*

"Very honestly and well written! Through *The Other Side of Grief*, grievers will see what worked well for the author in the midst of her unexpected and deep grief, a 'plan' that can give them hope. This is Carol Barnum's real story, written at a very personal level that many other grievers will easily relate to. I see this as an encouragement book that can help others know they are grieving 'normally' and direct them to rely on God."

— LINDA SIEGMANN,
GRIEFSHARE LEADER

"*The Other Side of Grief* will draw you into a story of love and loss, faith and grief. Carol Barnum shares the walk no one wants to take but everyone should prepare for: the sudden loss of one's best friend. For her, it was her husband Dave. People would ask her, 'Do you need anything?' Her reply, silent or verbal, was 'Of course I do, but for the life of me, I don't know what it is.' Carol's story shows how loss can tear a person's life into pieces, and how God can bring it back together again. Thank you, Carol, for being so transparent with us and helping so many walk this path!"

— DAVID H. HATCH,
SENIOR PASTOR, OUR SAVIOUR
LUTHERAN CHURCH, GREEN BAY, WI

"Grief is something that sooner or later will enter your life. This book will help you on that difficult journey with insight, inspiration, honesty, and faith in God expressed by Carol Barnum. She asked God who would ever want to read what she has written. God's answer to Carol was that he would give her the words to write, and when someone reads these words, they will hear what they need to hear. A must read for everyone!"

— KAREN BAIN,
ADMINISTRATOR, CARDINAL RIDGE
RESIDENTIAL CARE, GREEN BAY, WI

"Carol Barnum pairs her honest, heart-wrenching chronicle of grief with her abiding faith, which assures her of God's love, ever-present help, and eternal hope. She also offers readers practical advice about how to comfort and assist those in deep sorrow."

— JULIE KLOSTER,
AUTHOR OF *LEAPING THE WALL: PRACTICAL WAYS
TO EMPOWER FAITH IN DIFFICULT TIMES*

*The Other Side of Grief* describes what life is like through the eyes of a woman whose husband has died unexpectedly and gives helpful insight into the journey no spouse wants to be on. Even while the grief journey unraveled her inner being and everything she knew, Carol Barnum's faith in God and the Bible stayed strong. Through all her emotional and physical pain, her trust in God's plan for her life remained constant.

A phrase that stuck with me is, "Different is okay." Even though her husband isn't here and things have changed, Carol accepts that her current life is good; it's okay that it's different. She also describes ways friends can help those who are grieving when they don't know what to say to them. Overall, this book shows how trusting in God can help anyone go through anything.

— RENEE NATZKE,
BOOK REVIEWER

# THE OTHER SIDE OF
# GRIEF

*Why the Journey Matters*

## Carol Barnum

Deep River
BOOKS

The Other Side of Grief: Why the Journey Matters
Copyright © 2016 by Carol Barnum
Published by Deep River Books
Sisters, Oregon
www.deepriverbooks.com

ISBN – 13: 9781632694324
Library of Congress: 2016960473

Printed in the USA
Cover design by Robin Black, Inspirio Design

# DEDICATION

I lovingly dedicate this book to some very important people who have joined me on this journey. Thanks for being there.

* To Stacey, my outgoing and bubbly older daughter: You embrace life and dream big. Thanks for being you. I love you to the moon and back!

* To Brad: thank you —not only for volunteering to ride in the back of my little car and hold on to twenty-seven balloons, but also for giving Dave's football helmets a new home. You are awesome!

* To Kristen, the polar opposite of your big sister: You always have been your own person and you always will. Thanks for moving back home when you probably didn't want to. I love you infinity and beyond. Amen. (You win!)

* To my colleagues and office-mates—I love you all!

— Kay: Thank you so much for the endless prayer, support, and conversations.

You always knew when I needed a hug. Always remember to make every day a Tuesday.

— Linda: You are the one that always knew how I was feeling before I said a word. I love that about you. Thanks for keeping me honest.

— Deb: We have shared so much with each other about our lives and struggles.

Thanks for reminding me that I am not the only one in this world.

* To Brandon: You will always have a special place in my heart and in my life. You are an amazing young man! Thank you for the flag and for your respect.

* To Patti: You started on this journey before me and have helped me to navigate the bumps and potholes. Thanks for being someone who gets it.

And to the countless family, friends, and acquaintances that have been part of my life during this time: Thank you for your prayers, support, and for being there. Whether you knew it or not, you have been a significant part of this journey.

# TABLE OF CONTENTS

# INTRODUCTION

Let's get something straight right away: I never planned to write this book. It was never on my "to do" list. There is only one reason this book exists, which I will explain later.

Thing is: I don't pretend to be an authority on grief. However, I am the authority on *my* grief. While this book tells about my journey through grief and the many emotions and struggles I experienced, my husband, Dave, is a large part of this book. Many times I write "Dave's not here" or "even though he's not here anymore." What I mean is this: Dave is no longer living here on this earth in physical form. But he is here in every song, in every gentle breeze of the trees, in every melting ice cream cone. I can feel him every day. Memories of him live in my heart and the hearts of those who knew and loved him. And it is Dave's picture you see on the back cover. This picture of the two of us was taken in 2012, shortly after we became "empty nesters."

My prayer is that God uses this book to further his plan. I pray that as you read the words on these pages that God will open your heart and your eyes so that he may reveal his message to you. Different people may receive different messages while reading. That's okay. Different is okay.

# THE BASICS

For no one can lay any foundation other than
the one already laid, which is Jesus Christ.

1 Corinthians 3:11

These are some of the basic, or foundational, things I want you to
know about my life:

* I love my husband. He will forever be my always.

* I have never for a second doubted that Dave's death was
  God's will.

* I love my husband. I always have and I always will.

* Grief is the most difficult, confusing, exhausting thing I've
  ever experienced.

* I love my husband. There were a million little things about
  him that made our relationship special.

* I could never have gone through this without God.

* I love my husband. And I know he loved me more than anything in the world.

* I don't like roller coasters.

* I love my husband. He didn't like roller coasters either.

* Life is like a puzzle.

* I love my husband. That part, the best part of my life, is now dancing in Heaven.

* God is in control. He always has been and always will.

# CHAPTER 1

# Roller Coasters

*ups and downs*

Grief is like riding the most extreme roller coaster. In the dark. Blindfolded. It helps to remember that God is always in the seat right next to you.

> *So do not fear, for I am with you; do not be dismayed,*
> *for I am your God. I will strengthen you and help you;*
> *I will uphold you with my righteous right hand.*

> *Isaiah 41:10*

Every story has a beginning. This is where I will start.

On Monday, July 21, 2014, my husband, Dave, was brought to the hospital emergency room by a co-worker. It was determined that he had blood clots in his legs and lungs. He responded to treatments and medications and soon was acting like his old self. He was, according to one nurse, the least needy patient in ICU. One evening he rang for the nurse, and since this was so unusual, they came extra fast. But everything was fine. My husband just wanted to give them an update on the baseball score. That was Dave.

As we sat in his ICU room, we talked about everything. He would lovingly tease me and get under my skin just like at home. This familiar personality gave me a sense of security. At that point

I knew he'd be fine. He was in the hospital being taken care of by some great doctors. This was just a little bump in the road.

One of the things that gave me peace was the way Dave cared for me, even from his hospital bed. Five weeks before Dave entered the hospital, I had surgery on my foot to remove a bone spur and fuse the bones together in my big toe. So at the time I was wearing a black medical boot on my left foot and a tennis shoe on my right foot. I was still in the healing process, and I had to keep my foot elevated as much as possible. So even though Dave was in ICU hooked up to machines measuring his oxygen level, pulse, and blood pressure, he had a comfortable recliner chair brought in so I could put my foot up.

Dave spent Monday, Tuesday, and part of Wednesday in ICU, and I spent those days by his side. We talked, watched ball games, and talked and talked. On Wednesday he was moved to a regular room. Dave was responding well to the medication and getting better. I was so happy. But realistically, I never doubted the fact that he would improve. That evening I made my first-ever Facebook post. Other relatives and friends had posted updates on Dave's progress and requested prayer. On July 23, 2014, I wrote:

> *Dave has been moved out of ICU today and is now in a regular room. He continues to improve, and hopefully will be able to come home Friday or Saturday. Thanks so much for all your prayers and support.*

Just because something is written down doesn't mean that it will come true, but I didn't realize that at the time.

The next day the roller coaster started to warm up. I arrived at Dave's hospital room in time for the doctor to tell me Dave was being released. He was going home! We spoke at length about things Dave would need to do and watch out for.

Then Dave got up to use the bathroom, and I left to go get clothes for him to wear home. The last time I talked to my husband was through a bathroom door. I said, "See you later." I didn't realize, of course, "later" would be in Heaven.

When I was getting Dave's clothes, the doctor called. Dave had taken a turn for the worse. He'd have to go back to ICU, but in the words of the doctor, he was "out of the woods." As fast as my life started to rip apart, it was mended by just a few words. *He is out of the woods.*

After returning to the hospital, I heard a call for a medical emergency. But I was confident Dave was fine. But as I waited, a nurse and a chaplain approached me. Never good news.

The hospital staff did their best to prepare me to go into my husband's ICU room: There would be lots of people in the room, lots of different noises. They were doing chest compressions. What they didn't tell me was that my husband of almost twenty-nine years was already in Heaven. They weren't ready to give up yet. But the moment I walked into that room and looked at Dave, I knew he was dancing in Heaven. And probably playing endless rounds of golf.

The truly sad thing about this moment—the one thing I regret—is that I didn't tell the doctors to stop compressions. I knew it wouldn't make a difference. But I couldn't make the words come out of my mouth. The doctors finally stopped on their own.

Thursday July 24, 2014, 11:59 am: the moment my life was ripped in half. The moment that the roller coaster made its first drop. I'm so thankful that God was—and still is—in the seat next to me.

Everyone I called that day was shocked. No one had expected Dave to die. Some people cried. Some people just didn't want to believe it was true. God had taken a great man to Heaven that day.

Of course, the hardest calls were to my girls, Stacey and Kristen, who lived hundreds of miles away in different states. Thankfully, they had people nearby to help support them and make plans to get home quickly.

Originally Kristen's plane was to arrive that evening. Through a string of events, Stacey and Kristen ended up on the same flight the following morning. Not only that, but my daughters had seats next to each other. This was definitely God. He knew exactly what they needed at that moment.

Visitation for Dave was held on Sunday, July 27, 2014. The visitation itself was a roller coaster. I spent time with Dave before the others arrived. I said, "You weren't supposed to go anywhere." His skin felt hard, but he looked good.

I saw many people that night—some I didn't even know, who were kind enough to introduce themselves. Others I knew, but had not expected. More than once, as someone approached me, I put my hand up, gesturing to "please wait." I hope they understood that if I had not had those extra few seconds to get ready for what I knew would be a twist or a turn, I would have cried.

The funeral was the following day. Both my girls and I took turns speaking. In our own ways, we shared what was most important to us about Dave, and what we would remember most. For me it was a huge leap of faith. I don't like speaking in front of large groups. But on that morning, God spoke through me.

Our final good-bye came the next day at the mausoleum. We chose to release balloons at the end of the service. That morning I learned that my little car really will hold four adults and twenty-seven helium filled balloons.

After the service we went to lunch. To pay for the lunch, I used money Dave had been keeping in his wallet. I remembered several weeks earlier, I had asked him what he was saving for. He told me he didn't know, but he was sure something would come up. I'm sure this was not something he had ever considered.

Throughout the next weeks and months the roller coaster gained momentum and intensity. Sometimes it would move at warp speed as it twisted and turned and dropped. Then came times of relief when I moved on an even plane, but exhausting uphill climbs followed, along with the heart-stopping, gut-wrenching drops. I never knew when the downward spiral would begin or end. But I knew God was there every stop of the way.

## A New Life

For many months after Dave died I felt like I was living someone else's life. In the days after Dave died I would awake early and wonder, *Is this really happening? Is Dave really gone?* One year after his death, I woke up knowing that he was in Heaven *and* that this was really my life. I was also filled with a sadness so deep I knew only God could fill the void. Others could help, but only God could heal my broken heart.

> *He heals the brokenhearted and binds up their wounds.*
>
> *Psalm 147:3*

# CHAPTER 2

# WHAT SOCKS SHOULD I BUY?

*decisions*

> *What you decide on will be done, and
> the light will shine on your ways.*
>
> *Job 22:28*

There's a children's song about kids going on a bear hunt and facing and overcoming obstacles. The song starts out like this:

> *We're going on a bear hunt*
> *I'm not afraid*
> *Are you?*

The song continues as the kids arrive at several places that challenge them in their journey.

> *Coming to a wheat field/ deep cold river/ thick oozy mud/*
> *big dark forest*
> *Can't go over it*
> *Can't go under it*
> *Can't go around it*
> *Have to go through it!*

Grief is like that. You have to go through it. If you try and go over it, or under or around it, you will miss something. Probably something very important that God wants to show you. Yes, it is much harder to go through it. But it is worth it. You just have to make the decision to go through it. And then pray. A lot.

Seven months after Dave died, I pulled a muscle near my ribcage. As I sat down on a low stepstool in my classroom (I had done this dozens of times before) and tucked my legs under me (again, I had done it many times before), I heard a loud POP. I gasped for air and tried to breathe. Then I opened my eyes, and thought, *Please don't let me cry in front of all these four-year-olds.* And I didn't. I went through the rest of the day keeping my left arm close to my body and doing my very best not to breathe too much. Or too deeply. I still thank God that I did not sneeze that day!

At the urging of friends I went to see Dr. Mike, the chiropractor that I had begun to make frequent visits to (at that stage of my life I was on the every-other-day plan). The adjustment was helpful to relieve the pain of the pulled muscle, as were the ibuprofen and ice packs.

Unfortunately, this new development did nothing to help my already compromised sleep patterns. That night I woke up four times. The fourth time, at 4:30 AM. As I lay back, exhausted and in pain from my injury, I did the one thing I knew I shouldn't do: I started to panic.

The roller coaster was turning, and I wasn't ready. In my fear I cried out (literally) to God and said, "Lord. I am so tired! Please, please, please, PLEASE help me get back to sleep. I can't do this."

A peace washed over me at that moment.

Now let me make something clear: I've heard other people say the same words, but I never knew what they meant. I figured it was a saying to make things sound "religious." But it's true. A *peace* came over me. And then (this is the best part), God spoke to me, stopped me in my tracks. That morning I not only heard, but I listened. This is how the conversation went that morning:

> *Me: "Lord, what am I gonna do?"*
> *God: "My child, you can write a book."*
> *Me: "What?"*
> *God: "My child, you can write a book."*
> *Me: "Huh? How? I can't write."*
> *God: "All you have to do is get some paper and a pen. Put the pen on the paper. I will do the rest."*
> *Me: "Okaaaay. Are you sure?"*
> *God: "Yes."*
> *Me: (more confidently) "Okay, I can do that."*

From that point on, God gave me the words to write. If I stopped to think about what to put on the page, it didn't work. My mind would just go blank. And when I wondered who would ever want to read this, words failed me. It was when I reminded myself that God told me to write that the words flowed onto the page. So on February 26, 2015, I made a decision to listen to God. One of the best decisions since Dave died.

Take heart, my friend: the decisions have not always been this easy or clear.

> *Many are the plans in a man's heart, but it is God's purpose that will prevail.*
>
> *Proverbs 19:21*

## Small, Big Decisions

During the first few days after Dave's death, I, along with my kids, made a myriad of decisions. Which casket? What flowers? Which memory cards, candles, and thank-you notes? What days to hold the services and where? What times? How many boards do we need to make photo boards? What pictures should go on the photo boards? What color index cards to use for people to write their favorite memories of Dave? And on and on and on.

During each decision I knew God was there. Perhaps one of the most amazing decision-making experiences was when we went to the mall together to buy clothes for the funeral. My two daughters and myself each needed at least one dress. If you've ever been shopping with three women, you know what a challenge that can be. When the girls were in high school and needed a dress for a dance, we would start looking months in advance. We would search multiple stores in multiple cities. It took that much work. However, that day when we went to the mall, we each found one or two dresses at the first store we entered. And it happened in about thirty minutes. We could feel God guiding us.

In mid-August, I realized that I was still wearing my beautiful black medical boot. It was time to make the transition to wearing two shoes. My tennis shoes were the only option that would provide enough support for my foot at this time. But to wear a shoe, I needed to have the absolute thinnest socks possible. Since I only owned one pair of socks that fit this description, I went to the store to buy socks. It sounds like a relatively easy task, right? I stood in the aisle at the store and looked at all the socks. Some were definitely too thick, and I was able to rule those out relatively quickly. I had my options narrowed down to three or four pairs when I froze. I panicked. Right there in the middle of the store. All because of socks.

Grief had robbed me of my ability to make even the simplest of decisions. In retrospect, the worst part of the entire situation was that I had also forgotten to call on God, to include God in every aspect of my life. Socks.

*As for me, I call to God, and the Lord saves me.*

*Psalm 55:16*

You will be happy to know that I did buy socks that day. I ended up grabbing the ones with the best color assortment in the package. When I arrived home I found out that the socks I bought were too thick. I still have them, and I still like them. They were just not what I needed at that moment.

I wish I could say that after that exhausting, gut-wrenching experience I was able to turn to God whenever I had a decision to make or whenever I faced a challenge. I wish I could say that, but I can't. The good news is that God has always been there for me, before I call on his name and when I finally remember to turn to him.

This simple lesson with the socks made some of the bigger decisions easier down the line.

Like, when I made the decision to return to work in the fall. Many times during the year, I wondered how I would physically and emotionally complete my job. At one point when I was struggling with this dilemma, God assured me that I needed to be at work and finish the school year. It didn't make the rest of the year any easier, but I knew I was doing the right thing. I made a decision to trust God, and then reminded myself of this daily.

Other big decisions including going to a grief support group (which was scary! It stirred up many questions and emotions that I didn't even realize I had), redecorating my house, and taking trips to Rockford and Disney World with my daughter.

~~~~~

As I struggled to make big and small decisions, I realized that "staying in the day" was important. If I tried to look ahead to what I had to do later in the week, even tomorrow, it got to be too much. I struggled with this a lot. So many times I would rush ahead and plan what needed to be done next, guessing how something might turn out. In effect, I was borrowing trouble, playing the "What If" game. That is never, ever a good thing to do. I had to learn to focus on the moment. I still struggle with this, but I'm getting better.

There were many decisions that I had to make on a daily basis. Going to work was difficult at first, but over the months I learned that sometimes I just had to do it, no matter how I felt. In celebrating holidays, going out with friends, sharing my feelings, and even going grocery shopping, God taught me how to face each challenge, each decision. I learned to turn to God at these times, before I panicked and dissolved into a puddle of tears.

## Deciding to Let Go

Seven months after Dave died, I sat in the parking lot at a school and decided to "let Dave go." At the time, I didn't really understand what this entailed. But I knew I had to do it as I figured out what my life would be, as I put the pieces back together in a different way.

I finally realized that letting Dave go meant my heart was accepting that he was gone and never coming back, that I needed to build a new life. I had to let myself say good-bye. It doesn't mean I don't love him and miss him. Dave will forever be my always. Letting him go didn't mean that I will ever stop thinking about him and remembering the wonderful times that we shared together. It just means that I am ready for what God puts in my path next. I am ready for Him to show me the next step.

*Since you are my rock and my fortress,*
*for the sake of your name lead and guide me.*

*Psalm 31:3*

As it turned out, the next step was deciding to tell family, friends, and co-workers that my heart had accepted my loss. They needed to know that my tears were often for other things: the unknown, the changes, the loneliness. Then I could ask them to pray for God's guidance. But it was always a hard conversation to start.

I had talked earlier with my co-worker Linda, and she told me that she and the others in the office didn't always know what was going on at that particular time in my life—at what grief stage I was in. I had never thought of that, so I figured the best thing to do would be to share that information openly. And I did. I asked them to pray, but I got the feeling they had been praying all along.

By this time, it had been almost nine months since Dave had died. I had developed a closer relationship with God. During each step of the journey God taught me something. But I struggled with patience because I really wanted answers and results NOW. I tried to remember to take a breath and wait for God. He really does know what he is doing—even if things don't look clear to us.

I made many decisions during the months after Dave died. The most important decision was to believe God was in control and that he has a plan. It's true. Even through my tears and sadness, I know that God has a plan, something better than I could ever think of.

The Bible tells us that we do not have to understand everything that God does. We just have to have faith and believe. This has been hard for me. I want to understand the who, what, where, why, and how of everything. However, God wants me to trust that he has everything under control, so that is what I am trying to do. God has given me the strength and courage to explore the memories of my husband and best friend. With each passing day I am able to recall more memories, and have become more comfortable as I spend time taking that walk down memory lane.

# CHAPTER 3

# I Love You, but Please Just Go Away

*stamina*

Come to me, all you who are weary and
burdened, and I will give you rest

Matthew 11:28

Grief is exhausting. It takes every ounce of energy out of you. In the days after Dave died, I ran on adrenalin and autopilot. I was so blessed to have all the kids arrive home quickly.

Important terms to know:

Kids=Stacey, Brad, Kristen

Even though Brad was not officially part of the family at that time, I always have counted him as family and as one of the kids. I am proud to say that he and Stacey are now married, and Brad is my son-in-law. I couldn't be happier about that!

Girls=my daughters, Stacey and Kristen

At the time that Dave died, Stacey was 24 and living in Denver. Kristen was 20 and lived in Nashville.

I was even more blessed to have Stacey drive every time we went somewhere. That was one less stress factor to deal with at the time. It may seem small, but to me it was huge!

As hours turned into days, and days turned into weeks, friends visited. More often than not, they brought food. As a receiver of the food, I was thankful. It was one less thing to think about.

Here's where things might get a little sticky. Please don't get me wrong when I say this, and please don't let it keep you from bringing food or anything else to someone when they are in need.

I loved when people visited. I looked forward to it. I loved when people brought food. I needed to not have to think about what I was going to eat for dinner. I loved when I went out to lunch with someone, or anyplace else. I loved each and every experience. I would have said something if I didn't want to get together. But in all honesty, after about forty-five minutes, I had had enough. In my head I was screaming, *"I LOVE YOU, BUT PLEASE JUST GO AWAY!!"*

And then following it up, more calmly with, "I can't pretend to focus on what you are saying anymore, and I feel bad about that. I don't have any energy left to act like I care about what you are saying. And I feel really, really bad about that."

Right now I can picture people thinking, *Wait. How long did I stay when I visited? Did I stay too long? I hope not.* Rest assured, no one ever overstayed their visit. As I said, I loved when people came over. As long as they didn't stay too long. Because at the time I just didn't have the energy. Just "being" was tiring. So after each visit, I took a nap. God gave me rest.

## Get-Togethers

As hard as it was to be around people sometimes, God also used many of the get-togethers I had with friends and family, either immediately after Dave died—or in the year following—even if sometimes I only felt as though I were going through the motions.

At the end of Dave's visitation, a large group of fellow teachers came. We sat in a circle of chairs and talked. I sat in that circle of teacher friends and half listened as they talked. My mind was a million miles away, yet it was right there in the room. I tried not to look at the casket or the DVD that played continuous pictures of my husband. It was too painful. But the presence of my friends meant more than I even realized at the time.

After the funeral we went to Bay Beach, a small amusement park located in town. Somehow it seemed the right thing to do. Many relatives, including the young nieces and nephews went to Bay Beach that afternoon. I had debated about going with everyone. I was really tired and just wanted to sleep. But in the end I joined the others, and I am glad that I did. It was a great experience. Several of us, including me, even rode the roller coaster. It just seemed like the right thing to do at the time. But I still don't like roller coasters.

The week after Dave's death, I went to the Bullfrogs baseball game with Brandon (Dave's co-worker), and Lisa, his wife. Mountain Man from the TV show *Duck Dynasty* was there, and Brandon and I had our picture taken with him. Dave would have loved it. Brandon and I probably talked for half the game. Just remembering things about Dave.

Brandon had planned to take Dave to that game, but he never had the chance to ask him. So he invited me. At a time when spending time with people was sometimes difficult, it was never hard to talk to Brandon. He had worked with Dave for three years, and they had a special bond. He considered Dave his best friend. Brandon is now someone that I consider a good friend, and he holds a special place in my heart. As for who benefitted more from that evening of conversation and baseball, I did. But that's just my opinion.

Going to church was much harder than I imagined. One Sunday someone asked me how I was doing and that was it. I think she knew it was difficult for me, and we both steered the conversation in a different way.

I wish I could have answered that question. There was just no way possible that I could have done that without a waterfall of tears. Since then I have been able to prepare myself for that question. I'm not always honest about how I feel, but I am able to answer. As for church, it is still hard for me to be there.

God always knows what I need, whether it was to see someone in the grocery store for five minutes or to spend the evening with family. He used those encounters to help me grieve and to heal.

## Safe Places

Two months after Dave died, colleagues came into my office and simply asked, "How are you today?" At the time, I cried more than I talked. But as the months went on, I was able to talk more and cry less. But the one thing that never changed was the willingness of my co-workers to listen to me. I can't help but think that they got a little tired of my emotional roller coaster, even though they told me just the opposite. It was in my office that I was able to be myself. It was, and always will be, my safe place. Everyone should have a safe place, where they can just be themselves.

It took some time before my GriefShare group felt like a safe place. Many nights I didn't say much. I knew if I did, I might not make it through. I am, by personality, a quiet person. However, I have learned that there are times that I need to speak up. Since Dave died, I decided that there are three main reasons why I might not say anything:

1. I don't have anything to say
2. I have something to say, but I feel like no one would be interested

3. I have something to say, and I want to say it, but I know that if I start I would probably never be able to finish my thought. I would most likely end up in tears

The second and third reasons have been the most common reasons for me not speaking up. In fact, they are probably the most common reasons for all of us! My confidence was shaken greatly when my husband died, and there are times that I cannot imagine that anyone would be interested in what I have to say. Not only that, but often I am only one step away from tears. Sometimes just half a step. But I have learned that it is important to speak up and talk about Dave and my emotions. Even though there might be tears.

## Holidays

Kristen and I stayed home on our first Thanksgiving without Dave. There was no one else I would have rather spent the day with.

We had always spent Thanksgiving at home. Even though I had other invitations for this holiday, I wanted to stay home—per our tradition. But I did not spend the day cooking a huge turkey and an insane amount of potatoes as I had done in the past. Kristen and I watched the parade, ate pasta, and enjoyed chocolate pie for dessert. I decided I would be okay with making that our new tradition. We're taking it year by year.

Then, somehow, I made it through the first Christmas without Dave. A few days after Christmas I had Dave's family over to celebrate. It was wonderful to have a house full of people, but it was also hard. It helped to keep busy, making sure that everyone had everything that they needed. I was able to leave the room whenever I needed so I could "go check on something" or "go get something." In reality, I used those moments away from others to shed a few tears and take some deep breaths. Those quiet moments were exactly what I needed and gave me energy to continue on through the evening.

## Strength for Today

*Whenever and wherever.*

Sometimes when I think I'm too tired to do *this*, or I can't do *that*, I'm reminded that God gives me strength, and he will never give me more than I can handle. It's very humbling to think that God knows that I have enough strength for this.

*The Lord gives strength to his people,*
*the Lord blesses his people with peace*

*Psalm 29:11*

It still amazes me that God has chosen me for this journey, and I am so thankful for those that have stuck with me as I have traveled on this difficult path. I've found grief causes you to lose perspective on things, and the ability to think of others becomes difficult. Often I am so wrapped up in my own struggles, I forget there are people around me who are also facing difficulties. I am so sorry for that. I feel as though people have been there for me when I need it most, but I am not able to do the same for them. It feels selfish, and as much as I don't want to do that, the pattern continues. But in reality, I felt like a steamroller had run over me. It keeps going back and forth. Grief is exhausting.

During the times I had that steamroller feeling, I didn't feel like I was very good company. If someone invited me somewhere I would usually attend, but I was too tired to call someone and suggest that we do something. Let alone ask how they were doing.

Grief sucks all the energy out of you. During the weeks after my husband died, just existing exhausted me. But there were tasks, like laundry and cutting the grass, that had to be done. I often had to pick and choose what jobs I could tackle and which ones could be left for another day. There are some things, such as going out with friends, that I never wanted to say no to—even though

I knew that I would probably be extra tired the next day. It was always worth it.

Part of me realized that the lack of energy was a gift. I learned that in grief, it is important to spend time with others, but it is equally important to spend time alone with your thoughts and feelings. To be still. I'm still learning that.

In the end, I found going out or being with friends was crucial to my emotional well-being. It gave me a sense of importance, and helped me to feel that there was a purpose in my day-to-day life. Also it was fun. But I always wanted to make sure that in everything I did my husband was not forgotten. When it was appropriate I talked about my husband and shared about our lives together. Other times I thought about him and remembered the wonderful times that we had together.

After all, grief lasts a long time. During my journey through grief, I have been blessed with short breaks from the pain of my husband's death. These short breaks have allowed me to rest and re-energize. Each time the storms of grief returned I was able to navigate it with just a little bit more confidence. God has taught me to keep my eyes focused on him. He also has shown me that there will be times of rest.

*He stilled the storm to a whisper; the waves*
*of the sea were hushed.*

*Psalm 107:29*

Besides recognizing the importance of being with friends, I finally learned to listen to what my body was telling me. When I was tired or my head hurt I needed to put my head down and rest for a few minutes. When I was sad I needed to cry. Doing those things really did make a difference. It made me feel I could continue on with the day for a while longer. When I ignored the signals that my body was sending me I usually ended up feeling even worse. So my suggestion is this: put your head down and have a good cry.

From the moment Dave died, I knew God was in control and he had a plan. I never doubted that, but there were many times, I was just tired. Tired of waiting, tired of being strong, tired of the journey. Those were difficult moments, partly because I always felt like I should not have doubts. The best thing to do was to talk to God—about the grief, about my doubts—especially when I didn't feel like it. God strengthened me—even when I had doubts.

*Immediately Jesus reached out his hand and caught him.*
*"You of little faith," he said, "why did you doubt?"*

*Matthew 14:31*

## Still Learning

As I approached the one-year anniversary of Dave's death, I asked God what he was trying to teach me. To be still? To listen to him? I didn't know. I was confused. Although I asked, God didn't always answer right away. But I realized he was slowly teaching me patience. In the past I needed stamina just to exist, and now I also needed stamina to wait.

*But if we hope for what we do not yet have,*
*we wait for it patiently.*

*Romans 8:25*

# CHAPTER 4

# ON A SCALE OF 1 TO 10

*health*

*Are not two sparrows sold for a penny?*
*Yet not one of them will*
*fall to the ground outside your Father's care.*

*Matthew 10:29*

Not only does God know the pain we're going through, but he is there to catch us before we fall.

If someone had asked me after Dave died to rate my sadness on a scale of 1 to 10, I probably would have said something like 4,582. This puts things into perspective.

There are actually stress inventories that you can take to measure how much stress is in your life. So guess what I did? In the weeks after Dave died, I completed a stress inventory rating scale. Now obviously I knew that my score would be rather high. I was just curious to see how high it would be.

If you've never taken one of these, they are interesting, and also very subjective. I scored well over 300. Actually closer to 400. At the bottom of the test there is a scoring guide. A score of over 300 (remember, that's me) implies about an 80 percent chance of a major health breakdown or serious physical illness in the next two years.

I am a teacher of preschoolers, and in my job, germs are unavoidable. I honestly thought the reference to becoming sick meant that I was going to have one cold after another. So I stocked up on Vitamin C and multi-vitamins. I figured I would be safe with that. I will be the first one to admit that I was wrong. While I did have a few colds, what happened to me was different.

## Headaches and Sleepless Nights

I don't remember when the headaches started. I do remember that sleepless nights began when Dave died. The first few days after Dave died, I would go to bed at my usual time, but I would not get to sleep until 1 or 2 AM, then I would awaken about 5 AM. I laughed when I would get a call at 8 AM, and the person would apologize for calling so early. I had been awake for hours.

Of course, being tired—as I was—makes things about 1,000 times worse.

If I had to choose between having headaches the rest of my life or sleepless nights, I don't know what I would choose. But I need to sleep.

I have never quite understood sleep. It seems like it should be an easy thing to do—just close your eyes and go to dreamland. But it was never quite that simple for me, and my ability to sleep varied greatly. Without sleep everything always seemed more difficult, more intense.

Not two months after Dave died, I made my first visit to the doctor for a physical ailment. It would not be the last.

As the months dragged on, I slept less and less. Some nights only getting three or four hours of sleep. Even little things like clearing the driveway could cause stress and sleepless nights. Anything new—and, everything was new for me that year, as I had never done things like use a snow blower before—kept me awake. Throughout all of this God knew what was happening in my life and was watching over me. He knows and cares about every-thing—even the number of hairs on our heads.

> *And even the very hairs of your head are all numbered.*
> *So don't be afraid; you are worth more than*
> *many sparrows.*
>
> *Matthew 10:30-31*

## Lessons Learned

Falling asleep was often a challenge, so I tried to do things that would help with this. I have made it a personal rule to turn the TV off between 9:00 and 10:00 PM. It doesn't always help me to fall asleep, but at least I try. Sleep (or lack of it) has been part of my life since my husband died. There have been many ups and downs, and it is getting better, but in general, consistently having a peaceful eight hours of sleep is still a goal for me. I know it will happen eventually. In the meantime I have learned not to lie awake and listen for the garage door to open and for his car to pull into the garage.

And I have learned to put the panic that often arises when I'm over-tired in its place. Panic is a scary thing. It gives you a feeling that you are out of control. It's horrible. The panic in my life has subsided considerably, although I do have my moments. However, now I am able to recognize it for what it is. And breathe. Just breathe.

## Tears and Joy

In the same day, I could have tears and then happiness. Having a good morning at work was a momentous occasion. Since then I have even had full days at work that I considered "good." Not a lot, but it has happened.

But just like that, things would change. From having a good day to feeling overwhelmed and tired. The never-ending stress I experienced took a toll on my body and my life.

The February after Dave died, I finally admitted that my headache was constant and my sleep was compromised. At the advice of friends I took a step forward. I made my first visit to see a chiropractor. It was (and still is) a long process. But it has been well worth it. Each visit to his office provided a brief reprieve from the storms that raged inside me.

The luxury of sleeping more and having fewer severe headaches has helped to give me the strength to do the one thing that has been so important to me—to remember and treasure the memories of my husband and best friend.

## Healing

When God first told me to write a book, I wondered if writing wouldn't somehow help my sleeplessness and my headaches. The funny thing is: it really did. Writing helps me focus and stay calm. Occasionally on the nights I couldn't sleep, I took out my paper and pen. It may not have been the best choice, but at the time it was helpful.

The other thing that helped during those sleepless nights, when the storms kept coming, was holding on to God and his truths. Of course, some days were easier than others. But I began the practice of asking God *why* he wanted me to be awake, if there were something he wanted me to hear.

Those sleepless nights taught me a lesson: When I wake up, I need to remember to talk to God, and I need to listen. I have tried to do that ever since.

After beginning to visit the chiropractor, things started to improve. But I know that was not the only thing happening. Not only was I spending daily time with God and in prayer, but there were others who prayed for me. Just knowing that someone was praying helped me to feel stronger.

Unfortunately it was not a steady improvement. It was more like two steps forward, one-and-a-half steps back. Each one of those forward steps was an uphill battle. And with each step back-wards, I felt like I was sliding down a mountain. Some days it took everything I had to remember that God was in control. I had many tears during those backward slides down the mountain.

Still, there were many times that I had to ignore how my body felt and do what I had to do. This meant going to work when I was tired and not feeling well. This resulted in me becoming more tired, which really was not helpful. The only thing that got me through these days was to remember that God was in control.

*"I am the Alpha and the Omega," says the Lord God,*
*"who is, and who was, and who is to come, the Almighty."*

*Revelation 1:8c*

## Circular Grief

Grief is not linear. One does not go through Step 1 and then move on to Step 2. Grief is circular, and it does not seem to follow a pattern. Each stage is experienced over and over. There were times that I thought, *Phew, I'm so glad that is over and I am finished with that*. But things always came back for me to revisit again and again. The difference was that the second and third time around I was a little familiar with what was happening, and I was better able to face the challenge.

Within that space, I began to form difficult questions about my health and grief. I knew at least a portion of my headaches were due to stress, which was related to grief. Knowing that grief has no timetable and can last for years—or, never end—what does that mean in terms of having headaches? Will they always be there? I was afraid to ask.

I thought about that question for weeks before I was even able to write it down. I wanted to ask, but it was a scary thought. What if I didn't like the answer? And truly, can anyone really predict something like that with certainty? I figured that when I got up enough courage I would ask.

I was also really hesitant to tell people about my lack of sleep. I was concerned about their reaction. I could imagine people saying, "What do you mean you can't sleep? Just close your eyes." But whenever I started to fear their disappointment, I talked to God. He never disappointed me.

I could have taken a sleeping pill to help me sleep, but at some point I had to face the underlying cause of sleeplessness. I did try some over-the-counter sleep aids and did not like the feeling the following morning. I chose natural supplements instead.

Even still one night I woke up at 2:00 AM and I knew something wasn't right. It wasn't just that I couldn't get to sleep. It was that I was filled with anxiety. Close to panic but not quite. I would cry and then breathe. Cry and breathe.

I'm not exactly sure what caused that panicky experience. Sometimes it just happened, and when it happened at night the darkness always made things seem worse. But I had learned that I should take deep breaths. And sometimes crying was the absolute best thing to do.

It took a few weeks and lots of practice, but I was finally able to ask the question that I had wondered about for weeks: I asked Dr. Mike about my headaches. I was so glad that he answered honestly. He told me that as long as stress continued, they may not go away, but they could be reduced. That was what I thought, but it was good to hear.

It was especially helpful since I stayed so busy at work. With my grief and poor health, giving up before the school year ended would have been the easy thing to do. However, God had made it perfectly clear to me that he wanted me to continue working. He did not, however, give me clear instructions on what that would look like. So I went day by day, moment by moment, until the school year ended. Looking back on all that has happened, I can't believe I made it through. I also can't imagine how people can travel through grief without God by their side.

Many days during this time, I cried not because my husband died. At times my tears were for my physical pain. Of course, I still loved and missed my husband. But on some days I was in physical pain. It hurt, so I cried.

As I have written these words about health-related issues, I have always been somewhat self-conscious. I am aware that many people face bigger health struggles, but my only goal in all of this has been to describe what it has been like for me. While at the time that I experienced these struggles, it seemed like it was one of the worst things in the world, it really wasn't. It seemed that way because it was happening to me. I still have headaches and I still have trouble sleeping. But things are improving.

## Ignoring It

At one point, I decided I'd try to *ignore* the grief, the pain, the exhaustion. It may not have been the best idea, but I grew so tired of facing it. I was tired of facing the pain of grief. This included emotions, headaches, and compromised sleep. So in my frustration I decided to just push everything away and hope that this strategy was helpful. I went through the day ignoring my emotions and pretending that everything was fine. In all honesty I knew this would not be an effective way of dealing with things. But ignoring everything went well until the following morning when my emotions swallowed me up like an avalanche. I call it the crash-and-burn syndrome.

In reality all I did was avoid the pain for a brief time. Grief hurts. It *is* painful. There were times that if I stayed very busy and was constantly doing something, then I didn't have time to think about the death of my husband. Sometimes I kept busy on purpose. But the reality of it was, sooner or later I would have to slow down. I had to face the fact that I was no longer married and that my best friend was no longer with me. That was a very hard thing to do, something I still struggle with. But in the long run, pushing things away never changed my situation. It just meant that I was putting off dealing with grief.

By God's grace, during this time my sleep improved slightly and my headaches became less intense. I was able to focus more and concentrate. When I was able to get some sleep it helped me feel like a real person, not someone stumbling through life. But regardless of how much I slept on any given night, God gave me the strength I needed. And I am confident that it is only by the grace of God that I have been able to travel on this path.

*Your word is a lamp for my feet, a light for my path.*

*Psalm 119:105*

By May, almost ten months after my husband died, I was getting better at realizing that difficult times were not there to stay. Those rough patches were like waves in the ocean. They started out enormous, and if I allowed it, the wave would swallow me up. But if I remained calm, I was able to ride the wave, knowing eventually it would become calm again. God always knew how big of a wave I could handle at any given time. We didn't always agree on what size wave would be best for me at the time, but I knew that God would never let me fall.

Grief can affect every aspect of a person's life. That is why it is so important to address any concerns and difficulties as they arise. I certainly wish that I had done that. By the time that I admitted I wasn't sleeping well, it had been several months. Over time my sleep patterns slowly improved. At this point in my life, five hours was a long time to sleep without waking up.

Throughout this time, physical ailments just appeared, and I wasn't always sure of the cause. However, the day that I was bitten by a dog, I knew exactly what had happened. Once in the ER, it seemed like forever until they were able to give me something to ease the pain. As the medication started to take effect, I began to wonder why they called it a painkiller. It relaxed my body and took the edge off the pain, but it did not take the pain away.

That day I started to think about the pain in my hand from the dog bite and compared it to the pain in my heart. I knew my hand would heal quickly, and even if I were left with a scar, it would soon become a distant memory. The pain in my heart was another matter. I knew that over time the pain may become dull, and there will be scars, but the memory will always be close by.

And on the nights I can't sleep, memories, emotions, and fears always seem bigger in the dark. Even if it's pain from a headache that keeps me from dozing off, I am confident that it will not last forever.

Even with headaches and sleeplessness and grief, by the grace of God, I made it through the first year. God is good.

> *The Lord is good to all; he has compassion on*
> *all he has made.*
>
> *Psalm 145:9*

# CHAPTER 5

# THINGS DON'T GET BETTER, THEY GET DIFFERENT

## *changes*

*The end of a matter is better than its beginning,*
*and patience is better than pride.*

*Ecclesiastes 7:8*

Things don't get better; they get different. Before you get upset and think I'm crazy, let me explain my reasoning. To me, *better* implies that things go back to the way they were before. Like a mother kissing a boo-boo on her young child and saying "There, there. It's all better now."

Things will never be like they were before. So to me, it won't get better. But it will get different. Over time, the sharp pain that occurs after the death of a loved one may dull. I doubt it will ever go away. I cannot think of one aspect of my life that has not changed at least a little bit.

I love visuals and demonstrations. Please allow me to show you how my life has changed and what different looks like. (You can do this yourself to actually see what it looks like.) Take a piece of paper—any size, color, or shape. Now take that piece of paper and crumple it up, then open it again. Smooth out the paper with your hand. You will see creases and marks of different sizes throughout the page. Each line or crease represents something in our lives—something we liked, something we shared. It was all ours. Next take the piece of paper and rip it in half. This is how quickly the death of my husband happened. It gives new meaning to the terms "in the blink of an eye" and "like a thief in the night."

If this were all that happened things might not be so bad. Taping two pieces of paper back together isn't so hard. However, the first few days after my husband died, my life was slowly torn in pieces.

So, take those two halves of paper and rip them into small unequally sized pieces. Then take some of the pieces away, never to be used again. Next, mix up the remaining pieces. Taking away some of the pieces represented the death of my husband, and mixing up the pieces represented the upheaval that occurred in my life. Finally, blindfold yourself and try and put those pieces together to make a new puzzle. This is what happened in my life. At that point I knew that things would never be the same. They would never be better. Things would only be different.

Not only would things be different for me, but they would be different for those around me who knew and loved Dave.

Things would be different for Stacey. It meant that when she got married, she would not have her dad there to walk her down the aisle. That thought still leaves me with an ache in my heart.

Things would be different for Kristen. She wouldn't have her dad there on her 21st birthday. Her dad would never take her to another concert.

Things would be different for Brandon, Dave's co-worker, who took him to the emergency room and now had to go to work knowing that his best friend wasn't there anymore.

Things would be different for my neighbor, who no longer had his avid Packers fan and friend to go to Packers games with.

Things would be different for Dave's brother and sisters, as both their parents had already gone to Heaven.

Things would be different for the many nieces and nephews, some of whom had forgotten his real name and remembered him only as "Elevator Man" because of the way he used to lift them up in the air as an elevator does. And for the nephew born a few weeks after Dave died, his life would be different because he would never get to play with his Uncle Dave.

Things would be different for his best friend Jay. Never again would they be able to spend Memorial Day weekend on the golf course.

Different can be painful. It can be scary. But different can also be okay.

Things are different for me. I eat differently. And that's okay. I realized I don't really care about meatloaf, pork chops, green beans, and a lot of other foods. I only ate them because Dave liked them. I see things differently than I used to. My passion for life has changed.

## Changes

During our marriage Dave was the driver. He liked to drive. He drove to Florida, Maine, and Arizona on different vacations. He drove to Iowa to visit the Field of Dreams, and countless trips around the state of Wisconsin. He would drive anywhere. His favorite thing to do was to pull out his road atlas and look at maps of different states. A few weeks before he died, we had gone to Nashville to visit Kristen. Prior to the trip he studied his atlas and plotted a course that would take us from Green Bay to Nashville, then up to Ohio to see friends (and a few baseball games), return to Nashville and then back to Green Bay. He planned the route in ways that we would be able to see important sites, such as Churchill Downs and just about every ball field/stadium you could imagine. He drove because he liked it. And he was good at it. His sense of direction was impeccable. He had the ability to look at a map for only a few minutes, determine how to get to the destination, and then drive there without ever referring to the map.

As hard as Dave tried to teach me, I was never able to learn this skill. I am able to drive places with the assistance of written directions or a GPS. And I have become fairly adept at recognizing when I am going in the wrong direction (a skill that I have acquired only after much practice) and turning around and backtracking. So when I did things like make a short drive to the cinema in a neighboring town, it was an accomplishment for me. Things are different.

Dave was an early riser and always read the newspaper before he went to work. He usually returned home before I did, so he was the one to get the mail. These days the newspaper waits until I get home from work. That way I can get the mail at the same time-without forgetting either one.

These are some of the little things that caused me to feel like a different person. So I've prayed that I will be open to God showing me who I should be now. What I should do. God has a plan in all of this, and I want to make sure that I am doing what he wants me to do.

## Getting Used To Different

My first birthday without my husband came less than a month after he died. It felt different, and I tried not to think about what we had done on previous birthdays. Instead I enjoyed the time with family.

During the months after Dave died, I came to treasure the memories that I have, instead of just missing the fact that my husband was no longer here with me to create new memories. It has not always been easy.

And so, for a while after Dave's death, it was crucial I kept busy. But in doing this it did not give me a chance to spend time with my emotions, and it also did not give me time to relax. I still feel that need to keep busy at times, but not as much. There is a fine line between being busy and being *too* busy.

When my daughter Kristen's car died, she made the difficult decision to move back home. It may not have been what she wanted to do, but it made all the difference in my life. No longer would I have to come home to an empty house. God knew what he was doing.

Dave and I were creatures of habit, and for as long as I can remember we ate a light supper on Tuesday nights and ate popcorn as we watched television. The first time I made popcorn for myself it just didn't taste right. With Kristen home, I could enjoy popcorn night with someone else once again. Popcorn definitely tastes better with two people.

## Strength Through Heartache

Two-and-a-half months after Dave died, Brandon called to tell me his father had died. Brandon's dad was now in Heaven with my husband. And my heart broke all over again. I didn't know his dad, but I knew Brandon, and I ached for what he was facing. Over the next few months, I was faced with similar situations again and again. Several colleagues and acquaintances suffered the death of a loved one. Each time, my heart broke and I cried. Most of the people who died I had not known, but I knew the person left behind. I knew their lives were about to become very different.

Even as my heart broke for others in their grief, I felt as though I was not doing what I should. So I prayed that God would show me what he wanted me to do and to give me strength. But that was scary. Because to become strengthened, you must be faced with difficult things. And to ask God to show me his plan, what he wants me to do . . . well, you never know what that could mean. God could want me to do something completely different than what I am doing. Okay, so not so bad if it's God's plan. A piece of the puzzle. But it would still be different.

The Bible tells us to pray continually. I have not achieved that lofty goal. I try. I'm still nervous when I ask God to give me strength and to show me what he wants me to do, mostly because I don't know what he will tell me. But I am now confident that if God asks me to do something, then that's what I am going to do. It's just that sometimes God has to repeat himself until I listen and hear. And he does just that.

## Differences at Work and at Home

In the months after my husband died I often questioned my ability to effectively do my job. My co-workers tried to assure me I was doing a good job, but I still had doubts. It took some practice, but I was able to learn how to pretend to be excited about doing things, especially when I was in a classroom.

Getting work done in the house was a necessity. It was something that Dave and I had talked about but had never been able to complete. I am so glad that I was able to get this work done. I really like how everything looks. But most of all, it is mine. It's different. And that's good. But believe me when I say that Dave is in every part of this house.

So the December after Dave died, I experienced another first: Christmas without my husband. I still decorated the house, and the kids and I still went to church on Christmas Eve and opened gifts. We went to visit my family on Christmas Day, just as we always had. The Christmas celebration with Dave's family was at my house as previously planned. One of the saddest things about this was that the house was no longer our house. It was my house. Things were the same—but so different.

Over and over during this journey I have thought, *Is this really happening? It can't be true.* Even though I knew the truth, those thoughts found their way into my mind more than once. On New Year's Eve that year, I created a video of some of my favorite photographs of Dave. I watch that video often and I am reminded how things are different now. All I have left of Dave is photographs, memories, and love. It's different. Different can be scary and painful. But different is okay.

> *But as for me, I watch in hope for the Lord,*
> *I wait for God my Savior; my God will hear me.*
>
> *Micah 7:7*

## Juggling

That winter, I texted a friend to tell her that I couldn't juggle. That sparked a phone call in which I tried to explain my thoughts. The following week, convinced I had not effectively communicated my feelings, I sat with co-workers and again I tried to express my frustration at not being able to juggle. Here's what I meant: Good jugglers always keep their eyes on the things being juggled, not on their hands. For me, juggling means focusing on the important things in my life. I was able to verbalize the four most important things I was trying to juggle at the time.

1. My love for my husband and my journey through grief
2. My physical and emotional health
3. My family
4. My work

I explained that I needed and wanted to focus on each one of those things. If I set one of those down, I might never pick it up. Or worse yet, I would feel bad for not keeping my eyes on what was important. Today, I'm still not able to juggle, but I am able to accept this.

This helped me come to a realization, as I wrote in my journal:

> *So am I better? No, just different. Would I change*
> *anything? No. Because to change things would be to not*

*follow God's plan. And as much as it hurts, and is
painful and exhausting, I know God's plan is best.
The funny thing is, I feel like I may be on about step
seventeen of an infinite number of steps in this journey.
There's a whole lot more that will happen. But as long as I
keep on God's path, it will be okay.*

*And in all your ways acknowledge him,
and He will make your paths straight.*

*Proverbs 3:6*

This still holds true. Even if I could, I would not change anything. I would not wish to have my husband back for a few minutes, even if it meant I could have one more hug from him. Right now my husband is in Heaven, in a perfect place with no pain. If he were to return for one more hug that would mean that he would again be plagued with back and knee pain. Even if it were a possibility for that to happen, I could never ask him to do that. I love my husband too much.

Even the way I think of Dave is different now. I'm not trying to remember everything. And maybe because of that I am remembering so much more. Little tidbits of a memory, things he said or did, these thoughts and memories seem to wash over me. Not drowning me, but refreshing me. It's okay.

In fact, I love that I have more memories of Dave. Some bring tears, some bring smiles. It is such a relief to have peaceful memories. Those memories come to me wherever I am. Just the other day I was driving on a road that I travel frequently, and as I looked out the window, something triggered a happy memory from many years ago. Another day I saw a billboard and thought of the fun we had had on an anniversary date. It took almost twenty-nine years to build those memories, so I know there are a lot more special moments that I will recall in the future.

Life was wonderful when Dave was here. Even though he's not here anymore and things are different, I am so glad God chose me as the one to spend so many years with Dave. It is something that I will always treasure.

Like any marriage, not every moment was wonderful. But I have chosen to keep the memories of all the good times, and leave the not-so-good memories stored away. I can visit them if I really want to. I am thankful that I was able to spend so many years with Dave. I could wish for more, but I know that in God's eyes, Dave died at exactly the right moment. I am positive that God has a plan, one that is better than anything that I could ever imagine.

I've discovered this truth as I've gone back to look at my journal. Not only has what I have written changed but also how. It has been eye-opening to go back and re-read what I wrote in my journal. First of all, I can't believe that I experienced all of these things. Sometimes in the middle of our lives we miss some really important stuff. Going back and reading what happened and how I felt a few months ago has helped me to understand and to grow. I have gone from writing a laundry list of what I did, to expressing how I feel about my life.

Yes, my life is different. One year from now what will it look like? Where will I be? What will I be doing? I can't wait to find out the answers to these things. Taken all together, it's a wonderful life.

## Rebuilding

Rebuilding a life is hard because we don't know what it's supposed to look like. I don't have the written plan. How can you go somewhere if you don't have a plan? Trust. Faith.

> *Trust in the Lord with all your heart*
> *and lean not on your own understanding.*
>
> *Proverbs 3:5*

I like to have a plan when I do things and directions when I go somewhere. This journey has challenged me, because I only have God to rely on. Trust and faith.

I have never been one to read and study my Bible every day. For me, the Bible is very difficult to understand. And in the months after Dave died, I just didn't read. It took way too much concentration and focus.

But on one night in particular, I wanted to read my Bible. I wanted to search for what God wanted to tell me. I longed for some clues on God's plan. I still don't read every day, but it is getting easier to open up my Bible and read God's word. Even if I still don't understand what is written, God knows my heart and understands that I am trying.

Through this process I'm realizing how God has allowed me to rebuild my life.

I have come to love the life that God has given me since Dave died. That doesn't mean that I love my husband any less. I still miss him and am sad because he is no longer here. This life is different from the life I had with my husband, but that's okay. I cherish each memory I have of my husband and all the good times, and I also cherish each new friendship and experience I have had since he died. But I still wonder, *Why couldn't Dave be here for this?* By asking this, I do not mean to question why my husband died. I just wish that he could be a part of all the changes that have occurred.

If I think of my life as a book, I can see it as chapters. Since Dave died, I've been in a new chapter. I love the chapter in my life that Dave was a part of. And I want to keep re-reading that chapter over and over, and remembering and treasuring all my memories. But as I do that I need to continue to move forward. While frequent visits down memory lane are helpful, I know that remaining there would not be a healthy choice. It is necessary to move forward. My life is different, and it will take some getting used to. But that's okay. Different is okay.

The closer it came to the end of the school year and summer, the more I prayed about it. I knew summer would be a big change. Everything about my routine would be different, including who I saw and what I did. When I was calm I was able to believe completely that God was in control of everything. There were also times that anxiety crept in and the best I could do was to hope that I wouldn't be swallowed up by the huge change. I was extremely sad to say good-bye to my friends, co-workers, and office for the summer. While I definitely did miss the familiarity of going to work every day and seeing friends, I liked being able to sleep a little later and sit down in the afternoon and relax. Through all the changes and differences, God provided what I needed. That summer was different, and that was okay.

I also knew that the next school year would be different, but I was confident that God would prepare me for anything that He puts in my path.

*But you remain the same,*
*and your years will never end.*

*Psalm 103:27*

Just before the anniversary of Dave's death, I had gone to the beach to get away. I wanted something different, yet familiar. I chose to sit by the boat dock because that is one place that we had never sat. I was able to sit there under a shade tree and see the beach that we had visited many times before, but I was also able to watch the boats and create a new memory for myself. As I sat, I saw two parents with their young children venture out onto the pier and thought about how we had done that exact same thing as a family many years before. I became sad as I realized that our family of four was no longer together on this earth, and we will never again be able to take a walk together on the beach.

And yet, when I woke up that morning one year after Dave had died I knew that the day would be different. When Dave died, both girls had been living in different states. One year later Kristen was living at home, but Stacey was still in Denver. Months ago Kristen had asked permission to go to a concert on this day. I took a breath, thought of what Dave would have wanted her to do, and told her to get the tickets. I do not for a moment regret that decision. She had the best time she had ever had at a concert. At one point she texted, "Today is so good!! Dad's making this happen I can tell. I feel it." And I truly do believe that is the truth. The previous night Stacey was flying home from a business trip and looked out at the clouds and wrote, "I got to see the raw beauty that we are surrounded by, day in and day out." I am so blessed that my girls have assurance that their dad is in Heaven and is watching over them. So even though it has been a difficult year and things are different, I am so happy that I know that God never changes.

*Jesus Christ is the same yesterday and today and forever.*

*Hebrews 13:8*

# CHAPTER 6

# PEOPLE SAY THE DARNDEST THINGS

*things people might say*

*Do not let any unwholesome talk come out of your
mouths, but only what is helpful for building others
up according to their needs, that it may benefit
those who listen.*

*Ephesians 4:29*

Let's face it, when someone dies, no one knows what to say to the person left here on Earth. Most people want to say something, but there is no guidebook of what to say when someone dies. And it wouldn't really matter if there were a guide, because everyone is different. Everyone reacts differently to the death of a loved one. Here are some things that people have said to me (either directly or indirectly), what I thought about those words, and how I responded (or how I wanted to respond):

Q. *"Are you feeling better?"*

What I often said was, "Yeah, a little bit." What I really wanted to say was, "No, I am not better. My husband died. My life has been torn apart. I am not better. But I am different. So if it will help to change the topic any quicker, I will go ahead and say that I am feeling a little better, because I know that's probably what you want to hear. It's too hard to explain anyway."

### Q. *"How's it going?"*

What does that even mean? This question can be answered on so many levels. Are you asking me where I am in the grief process? Or are you asking me if I had a fun weekend? Or are you just asking "How's it going?" because that is a reflex greeting that people use, and you don't really expect an answer? Do you really care how things are going in my life?

This has been a hard question for me since Dave died. I was never really sure how much information people wanted, so most of the time I just answered "okay" and walked on. There were some people that knew when I wasn't being honest and would question me. And I was perfectly okay with that, because I knew that they really cared.

### Q. *"Do you need anything?"*

Of course I need something. But for the life of me I don't know what it is. And if I tell you that I need something, it will make me even more vulnerable than I already feel. I would have preferred that people guess at what I needed. Because whatever they would have guessed, I probably would have needed it. And I definitely would have appreciated it.

### Q. *"Good morning."*

Yes, I realize that is not a question. But I didn't like those two little words. Not for a long time. At first after Dave died, my reflex was to repeat those words whenever someone greeted me with a "good morning." After a while, I realized I really didn't like what I was saying, so I made a conscious decision not to say good morning. When someone said those words to me I responded with a "Hi" or "Hello."

I know this is a little thing, but unlike "good morning," it was from my heart. Seriously, what was good about the morning? I don't know if anyone ever noticed. After a while, I was able to start answering people with a "good morning." But only when I truly felt that way.

## Q. "Are you okay?" (said with rising inflection)

This question is like "How's it going?" Do you really want to know? Do you have that much time to listen to me and hear me? Some moments I was able to answer yes and really mean it. Granted, it took months to be able to do this. More often that not (if I was being totally honest with myself and others), I wanted to scream, "No I am not okay! I am scared to death that I am doing a lousy job at work. I am scared that I will never stop crying unexpectedly. I am scared that I am not spending enough time with my girls/ Dave's relatives/Dave's friends helping them with their grief. I am scared that I will never again be able to read a paragraph in the Bible and understand it. I am scared that I will never be able to juggle. I am scared." But most of the time I just answered by saying, "Yeah, I'm okay."

To those select few of you who listened to me and heard me when I talked about these fears, thank you. Words cannot express how deeply loved I felt at those moments.

If you ever asked me any of those questions, take heart. I never once took it as a sign that you didn't care or wanted to hurt me. Trust me, if it bothered me at the time, I took a breath and then let it go. I told myself to shake it off. Believe me when I say that I've spoken those same words in similar situations. Because no one really knows what to say when someone dies.

There are some things that people said that I really did appreciate, as well as things that I thought would be helpful for me. Here they are:

As a general rule, ask specific questions. Open-ended questions require a higher thought process and are much more difficult to answer. When you add grief to the equation, open-ended questions can cause considerable amounts of anxiety. For me, yes, no, or multiple choice questions were a little easier to answer. Here are some examples.

- "I noticed that your lawn needed cutting [or driveway needed shoveling or anything else]. Can I come over this afternoon and take care of that?" A simple yes or no answer is all that is needed. But beware: when people asked me that question, I often said "Oh, you don't have to. I can do that." I was grateful, and yes, I wanted the help, but it made me feel even weaker and more vulnerable. So when you hear that, tell the person, "I know I don't have to, but I want to. I'll be here this afternoon." They will love you for it.

- Notice something. Then wait. Say "You look tired" or "This must be hard for you." Then pause. Wait. Those words are statements. They do not require an answer. But those are the things that I was able to respond to most easily. That is, after I remembered to take a breath and wipe away the tears from my eyes. Those types of statements assured me that the person speaking to me cared enough not to expect anything in return.

- "Are things working out with _____ [anything specific: carpet installation, job task, anything at all]?" Again, a yes-no question. I liked those types of questions, because I knew exactly what the other person wanted to know, and I could answer yes or no. If I wanted I could elaborate, but I didn't have to.

- "We should go out to dinner/to a movie. How about Saturday?" When people said this to me, I knew what was going to happen, when, and where. That meant limited decisions on my part. If you offer something like this, please follow through. I had someone make a similar offer, but the time-line was "some time." I have never looked at a calendar and seen a day called "some time." In this particular instance, the suggested event never took place. And while there is a lot that I don't remember (it's called brain fog), that invitation was as clear as could be. I'm still a little sad that the event never happened.

- Talk about your life, something that you did. Believe it or not, it was (and still is) a relief to not always have to think about what was going on in my life. My life is exhausting. And many times I've wondered if people get tired of hearing about my struggles. There were many times that I would have preferred to listen to someone tell me about their kids, their grandchildren, their struggles. It gave me a brief escape from my own challenges and changing life.

- "What are you struggling with right now at this moment?" I don't think anyone ever asked me this question, but there were times that I wished they had. This is a hard question to answer, but it is specific. Be prepared for the answer. And only ask if you really want to know.

At Dave's visitation, Stacey's friend Meggie came up to me, gave me a hug, and quietly said, "Thank you for being such a strong mother to Stacey and Kristen. You are doing an amazing job!"

Sometimes people, without even planning to, say something so honest and from the heart that it brings you to tears. That is exactly what happened to me that evening. I will never forget those words. Months later Meggie told me that the words she spoke that evening were not planned or rehearsed. She gave me a hug to comfort me and the words that came out of her mouth were clearly from God. Those words that were said in love brought happy tears to my eyes that night.

Another time, I expected a promised call from a friend and it didn't happen. I felt crushed by the broken promise. These feelings occurred with such intensity that they nearly brought me to my knees. My emotions were running over me. I asked God to forgive me for my anger, and in my heart I forgave my friend. I could not tell my friend how I felt though. I did not want my friend to feel bad.

Many months after Dave had died, I walked into my office, and as I approached my desk, I saw a beautiful pink envelope on my chair, my office-mate's handwriting visible. My heart skipped a beat because I knew that whatever was inside had the potential to spark emotions in me. I sat down, took a deep breath to prepare myself, and opened the card. Inside I found a beautiful, "We think of you often and pray for you" card. These women had witnessed the difficult storms that I had been experiencing that week and wanted me to know that they would always be there for me, no matter what.

The significance of this was not only that my colleagues said they cared, or that they listened to me when I was having a challenging moment. The significance was that seven months after my husband's death, they were still doing these things. I knew they would be there for as long as I needed their support. They understood that grief was as unpredictable as the weather. I will always love them for that, and I will always be there for them whenever they need anything.

Other times, people said things that rubbed me the wrong way. It just happened and I usually tried to let it go. I tried to take it with a grain of salt. But it was hard some days.

Then there were times people would say or do something that assured me that they were, in their own way, trying to help, trying to fix whatever they perceived to be wrong. And I let them. Because it was very thoughtful of them, and it meant something to me. And maybe, just maybe, there was part of me that hoped that their words or actions would help fix things. Because at that moment God was telling me to wait and I was getting very impatient.

*I wait for the Lord, my soul waits,*
*and in His word I put my hope.*

*Psalm 130:5*

But it wasn't just the questions and comments that got me down. One of the many hard things about grief (besides the obvious) is getting used to, and accepting some of the language, things specific to having a spouse/loved one die.

* *Widow*: I hate that word. The more I hear it I still don't like it, but I'm not afraid of saying it anymore.

* *One-year anniversary*: I never understood why people talked like that and why it would be so significant. I get it now.

* *Marital status*: I hate answering that question. It wasn't my choice.

* *Loss—as in she lost her husband*: I understand the meaning of this and if others want to use this term that's fine. But I do not like this because it is not true. My husband died. I did not lose him. I know exactly where he is. He is in Heaven, probably in the sports room. But I did not lose him.

Grief is what happens when someone you love dies. With grief comes some very uncomfortable changes. Answering questions regarding marital status and updating current information have been a few of the less desirable things that I have had to deal with. I know there will always be difficult situations that arise, but I prefer to not look ahead and think of the "what ifs" more than I should.

## Choosing to Say Nothing

Somewhere in my journey, I realized I didn't have to say anything. Sometimes the best thing to say is nothing. There have been numerous times that I wanted to say something, but the words would not come out . . . yet. Emotions overtook me, and I struggled between wanting to express myself and just giving up.

There have been some very perceptive people who have understood this at the exact moment and will wait. They say nothing with their mouths, but their body language says they are willing to wait an eternity if needed, just so they can be there to listen. This patience has allowed me to gather my strength and talk (even though it is often through tears).

There were times I would choose not to share what was happening, and that was okay too. Whether it was because I didn't feel like crying at the time, or if it was because I needed time to think about and process things, I wasn't always sure.

In the months after Dave died, I knew many people who experienced the death of someone close to them. I attended several visitations and also a funeral. Even though I had experienced the death of someone very close to me, I still didn't know what to say. I knew which words were helpful to me and which words were not. But I still had difficulty coming up with the right thing to say. So if you need to, go ahead and ask "How are you doing?" But if you ask, please be prepared to listen.

## Conversations

I like to have conversations with people—even when they are not there. Sometimes it's a continuation of what we talked about; sometimes it's a question I have. For example, I might ask:

*My Q: Why can't I sleep?*

*Response: What do you think?*

*Me: I don't know. It should be easy to sleep.*

*Response: Has your sleep gotten better?*

*Me: Absolutely! I no longer sleep for forty-five minutes and then lie awake thinking about Dave and other things.*

*Response: So that's good. Your sleep is improving.*

*Me: Well, yes, but how long will it be before I can sleep all night? Why can't I sleep all night?*

*Response: How long has it been since you've been having difficulty sleeping?*

*Me: Eight-and-a-half months.*

*Response: And how long has it been that your sleep has been improving?*

*Me: About one-and-a-half months*

*Response: So...*

*Me: So you're saying that it took a long time to get to the pattern of sleep that I had. And I shouldn't expect to see everything back to normal right away.*

*Response: (smile)*

The nice thing about talking to people when they are not around is that I can control the conversation. In a world full of uncertainties, that is an unbelievable power to have. This conversation wasn't with anyone in particular. It was just something I wondered about.

The other reason I had conversations with people when they were not around was so that I could practice my answers. I would think of potential questions that I might be asked, such as "How are you today?" or "Are you okay?" and then decide how I would answer. It might not make sense, but it helped ease some of my anxiety.

## Communicating without Words

One day as I was talking to my friend Kay, she gave me a hug and I just cried. Partly because I was so tired. But I think part of it was the hug. A hug.

Sometimes people said things that touched my heart. There were also times that words were not needed. Often a pat on the shoulder or a hug meant more to me than a million words.

It's amazing how much can be communicated without words. Something like a hug speaks volumes.

So does caring enough to tap on your car window when you're inside crying, and not worrying that they might startle you. They just want you to know that they are there for you. This is what a friend did for me one day.

Yes, I was crying again. Tears were a large part of my life, but I often tried to hide them from others. After all, I never wanted anyone else to feel uncomfortable. In this case, I had left a meeting and had just barely made it to my car when the tears began. I closed out the world around me and sobbed, pouring my heart out to God. When my friend gently knocked on the car window, I knew that it was not a coincidence that she walked past my car when she did. God is always hard at work, placing people at the right place at the right time. She knocked on the window because she cared, and because of that one small gesture I knew God was telling me that I was loved, and he would give me the strength to continue with the day.

I realize I like everything about my new life except that my husband is not here to share it with me. That makes as much sense as the doctor who told my daughter, "For a sick person you're really healthy." If my husband were here, I would not have a new life. I would be living my comfortable, safe, secure life that I had with him. Moving forward while still honoring and treasuring the memories of my husband has been confusing. So many variables are present, and they change from day to day. I think it is possible to embrace your new life while you look back and remember all the good times, but it is also easy to become stuck in grief and to play the "poor me" game. Being sad is part of grief, but rebuilding your life without your loved one is also part of grief.

During the past year, the best things anyone ever did for me were to wait for me, listen to me, and tell me that they were praying for me. Along the way there have been many people that have done all three of those things for me. There were people who waited as I took deep breaths and wiped away tears, listened as I stumbled over my words and tried to express my feelings at the time, and told me they would pray for me. Often in return, all I could say was thank you, because I knew if I attempted to speak any more the words would very likely get stuck in my throat and the tears that were in my eyes would fall onto my cheeks.

There were days I felt sad. But there were also days I felt so blessed. I have so many friends and family who have supported me every step of the way along this journey. I have people who have prayed for me, listened to me, and cried with me. People who have been there no matter what. My husband died but God is still providing me with endless blessings.

*Those who sow in tears will reap with songs of joy.*

*Psalm 126:5*

## CHAPTER 7

# TIE YOUR SHOES, DEAR FRIEND

## *faith*

*You need to persevere so that when you have
done the will of God,
you will receive what he has promised.*

*Hebrews 10:36*

One of my favorite songs is "Press On" by Billy Sprague. It speaks of being in the valley of the shadow of death and how spiritually, emotionally, and physically exhausting that is. The words in the song tell of praying for relief from the storms in life, but feeling as though prayers are either being ignored or refused. It describes how some days it feels like all you can manage to do is to tie your shoes.

And that is faith: tying your shoes, and accepting that may be all that you can accomplish at that moment. I have felt that way many, many times.

As I sat in the ICU waiting room the day Dave died, I was approached by a nurse and a chaplain. As they explained what was happening with my husband, I asked if I should call my kids right away. They said, "Let's just take one thing at a time." Those were very wise words. I quickly learned that if I were to keep it together, I needed to focus only on the present and not look ahead.

At first I needed to take this very literally. There were days I thought, *I am eating my breakfast. That is all I have to do. Just eat breakfast.* If I jumped ahead and considered my long list of stuff to accomplish that day, I would become riddled with anxiety. There were times that even the thought of having to wash dishes caused my body to stiffen. I have had lots of dirty dishes that sat in the sink for days. Eventually they always got washed. Sometimes they just had to wait awhile. But that was okay, because at the moment all I had to do was tie my shoes.

The song also speaks of having heavenly friends. I have been truly blessed to have friends like this. Heavenly friends who have carried my heartache and made it their own. Friends I could lean on. Friends I could call at two o'clock in the morning, or nine o'clock at night. Or whenever I felt as if I needed help to press on.

I have learned many things from my friends: effective ways to help kids learn, resources when helping families, and insights about God. But perhaps the most important thing I learned was how to breathe and feel my emotions. Whenever I was having a difficult moment and struggled to exist, my friend, Kay, would look at me and calmly say, "Breathe. Just breathe." There were times that she would breathe for me until I was able to conquer this insurmountable task. And then she would breathe with me, as only a friend can do. (Thanks Kay, for teaching me how to breathe.)

Even though I had learned how to breathe, there were many difficult days. There were also many, many times that I would be feeling relatively strong (I got pretty good at pretending to focus and not cry) and then something would happen. Anything. In August, a few weeks after Dave died, I received an e-mail letting me know that my supervisor, whom I had known and worked with for years, was taking another position in the school district. It was a wonderful opportunity for her, and for that reason I was happy for her. Even so, I cried at this change in my life. I was so sad. God reminded me to tie my shoes.

## Waiting for the Good Parts

I like to read. During the school year, I don't usually have enough time to enjoy reading a good book. However, once the school year ends, I start my frequent trips to the library. Afternoons are often spent sitting on the patio in a comfy chair, book in hand. I am usually very choosy about the books I read, and if they don't grab my attention within the first few pages, I trade it for another book from the library pile. This is one time that I did not have that choice. No matter how I felt, this book, the things that were happening in my life, was not one that could be put aside. I would need to continue. As I wrote in my journal just before going back to work after Dave died: *I am concerned about going back to work. There are times that even small decisions send me to anxiety. Then I remember to breathe. I am almost excited to see what God has planned. The other part is really sad and wonders what is so significant that God did not want Dave to be here for it.*

My concerns were justified. That school year was rough. Very rough. Definitely the most difficult year that I have ever experienced. There were many times I didn't know if I would make it through, and then I would be reminded to press on. I still get excited at times to see what God has planned for me. To see what is next on the path that he has prepared for me. And I still get sad, because Dave is not here to share these things with me.

At the end of August summer break ended, and I returned to work. During the first few weeks there was a hint that we might have to move to a different office. Just the idea brought fear to the front and center in my mind. I looked at my co-workers and very calmly (actually with terror, and tears ready to spill over) told them, "If we have to move I will cry." I don't know if they realized how very serious I was at that moment. At that time there were giants in my fears. I had to press on.

I still have days that I am overwhelmed, and I also have days in which I doubt my abilities to successfully do my job. I have been assured by co-workers on numerous occasions that I am doing a good job. As for enjoying my job, I have had many, many moments that I have enjoyed myself. I have many wonderful memories of the good things that happened, and when I start to doubt myself, I try to think of the positive things that have occurred.

> *Blessed is the man who perseveres under trial; for once he has been approved, he will receive the crown of life which the Lord has promised to those who love Him.*
>
> *James 1:12*

It was amazing how, just when I needed it most, God put someone in my path. Too often—especially when I'm tired—I look to what I am missing, and what I don't have. But these people who show up remind me to look at what I do have, and the many blessings God has given me.

Just as God puts people in my path, he also allows me to spend time with myself and my thoughts, even when I don't think that is the best solution to what is going on at the moment. There have been many times that I have struggled with something and wished that someone would call me—or just magically appear. At first when nothing happened, I would become disappointed, only to realize that there was someone there. God was there! And at that moment he wanted me to turn only to him and to discuss my current struggles with him. He wanted me to have faith.

Even so, I still don't like uncertainty and the unknown. And I'm still not sure how I should feel about a lot of things, even though I know there is no right and wrong when it comes to emotions. What I have learned over the months since Dave died is that the best thing to do is to hold on to God's hand, pray, and listen to God. Sometimes I think the listening part is the most important. Listening to God is what helps me discern what God wants me to do—and hearing his voice gives me the strength to do it. As does knowing that God walks with me in my grief.

One day not long after Dave died, I imagined God walking next to me, holding my hand. It was so nice. I still do this. It is the most wonderful feeling. So if you ever see me walking, and I have my hand closed (not a clenched fist, which usually means pain or a very intense memory), I am probably holding on to God's hand. You should try it.

But I do wish God would be clearer in his communications with me. I wish I could have a progress report to find out how I am doing. Or a postcard in the mail. But I know God doesn't work that way. He wants us to have faith and to trust him. That is so much harder to do! But I also have learned that the more you talk to God and trust him, even in little things, the more he will show you about the bigger things.

Faith is a tough thing. We want someone to tell us we're doing the "grief thing" the right way. Of course it never happens, because there is no right or wrong way to experience grief. And when I accepted and realized that fact, then there was one less thing for me to wonder about. But I didn't always remember.

## Overwhelmed

A few weeks before Christmas, I wrote in my journal: *Lord, please teach me to be still. There are so many things in my life now, and I am becoming overwhelmed. I want to retreat and avoid all these things, including work. But I know that is not what you want me to do. I know you want me to take your hand and face these things.*

I was overwhelmed. Often. Many times I wanted to crawl under the covers and stay home. And sometimes I did. But as the school year progressed, I used fewer sick days. I became better at time management while I was at work. And even though there were times that I wondered about it, I continued to work full time throughout the school year. Because I was absolutely positive that was what God wanted me to do. I took God's hand and faced what was before me.

For whatever reason, I felt like I had to be strong, like I had to show to people that things were just fine—even when they weren't. Guess what? That type of approach just does not work forever. Those that were closest to me knew the truth, and I poured my heart out to them. They tried to convince me that I didn't have to be strong. God knew the truth, and he was waiting for me to admit that I wasn't as strong as I wanted to be. But I still try to be strong. I guess God's not finished with me yet.

*He gives strength to the weary and increases*
*the power of the weak.*

Isaiah 40:29

The first winter after Dave died, I thought things had been going along somewhat well. But then I had my "blindfold" removed. It was a startling experience. All of a sudden, I could see things more clearly. I felt like I had to make up for lost time. In addition to feeling like I always needed to be strong, I also felt like I needed to give 110 percent at my job. And spend time with my family. And keep the house clean, the laundry washed, and all the other things that go along with maintaining a house. And spend quality time with God. And spend time with my thoughts and memories. I wanted to be able to do it all, but I couldn't. I have since come to accept that if the carpet doesn't get vacuumed as often as I was hoping for, that's okay. If the clean dishes sit in the dishwasher an extra day, it doesn't really make a difference. If I didn't finish everything at work, it would still be there tomorrow.

What I could never compromise on was spending time with God, and also with my thoughts and memories. Those were the really important things.

It was six-and-a-half months before I felt that the first layer of the blindfold was lifted. Six-and-a-half months. That is a long time to be in the dark. Throughout this time I had been moving along, walking purely with blind faith. While it was nice to be able to see some things that I had not noticed before, it was also a little scary. The comfortable pattern that I was used to was changing yet again.

I was reminded that staying in the day is important. If I try and look ahead to what I have to do later in the week, even tomorrow, it gets to be too much.

Over time, my ability to stay in the day has gotten better. I can look ahead to things. Sometimes there is anxiety, but at least I understand why. Sometimes I can't spend too much time thinking about the future. I just can't stay there. Because I know that God already has all that figured out and he knows what is going to happen. So I shouldn't spend time thinking about what might or might not happen. It's better to think about now.

Though I still wake up in the night—sometimes in a panic. But again, I remember to talk to God, and ask him why he wanted me to be awake at this time. God has a reason for everything. Even for waking me up at night. Sometimes that was the only time that I was able to listen and to hear God—the rest of my life was so chaotic.

Some days I feel I am being bombarded by words from God, giving me words of encouragement and strength. This is a good thing, although sometimes I felt overwhelmed by so much coming at me at one time. I knew that through everything God had never left me, he had never forgotten me. He was just waiting for me to hear. I have received so many encouraging words from God, so many words of wisdom. Please don't get the idea that from this point on I didn't have doubts or fears. Those were abundant. But I also had God whispering in my ear, telling me he loved me and that he had a great plan for me. He was probably telling me this all along, but now I could hear. I'm so glad that I had faith, even when I couldn't hear.

## A New Life

Perhaps one of the most difficult aspects of this journey has been getting used to my new life. I am no longer a couple, no longer Dave's wife. I am getting used to my new life without my best friend by my side.

I know now that nothing is certain. Things can change in the blink of an eye. I also know that God is in control, and he has a plan. That I am sure of. And I know that his plan is to prosper me and not harm me. I am sure of that. What I don't know is the details of his plan. That is the scary part.

Before Dave died I did not realize how fast a blink of an eye was. Now I understand. Because his death happened so quickly, I had not had time to prepare for it. Because of this I look at many things differently.

For instance, I have always worried about my kids when they traveled, but this trait intensified after Dave died. If a friend or family member traveled, I worried. I'm not saying that it was the right thing to do, but that is what happened. Worrying never helped. God has since shown me that it is better to have faith that he will protect those who are sick and traveling, and that his plan will be carried out. This was difficult for me to accept at first, because I knew his plan could include things that I didn't like. The more that I prayed about this, the more God gave me the strength to follow him.

*Therefore do not worry about tomorrow, for tomorrow will worry about itself. Each day has enough trouble of its own.*

*Matthew 6:34*

Even as I tried not to worry, I found myself wondering, *How do I fit everything in? How is it possible to do everything that I need to do and everything I want to do?* The answers, of course, were faith, trust in God, and patience.

Even though I believed that everything that happened was part of God's plan, it was hard to face the fact that I just didn't have the energy to do everything that I needed and wanted to do. That frustrated me. I could accept that my husband died, but I needed to learn to face all the little things. This took an extraordinary amount of faith—something that I didn't always have.

And then there were days that I needed help to tie my shoes. I knew that I could ask God and he would always be right there for me. I will never understand why God has chosen this path and these obstacles for me. But I do know that the more I turn to God and trust him in every situation the stronger I become.

Although true, I'm sad to admit this: there were many times that I knew what I should do, but I just didn't want to do it. I felt that it would take too much energy and too much courage. If I had just asked God for energy and courage for that one task I faced at the moment, perhaps things might have gone a bit more smoothly. Perhaps.

*Put on the full armor of God, so that you can take your stand against the devil's schemes.*

*Ephesians 6:11*

When someone you love dies, and you are experiencing grief, this is what you need to do. Put on the armor of God. And get ready for the battle—and great lessons—of your life.

I really wanted to know what the objective of the lesson was. Tell me what the goal is and then I can do it. But God does things differently, and I believe some lessons are meant to teach me that

I am not supposed to understand everything. I am supposed to have faith and follow God. No matter what.

I was able to understand that Dave's death was God's will, but it didn't make sense that smaller things could be God's will. I struggled with this for a while, then decided that I just needed to have faith and trust that God was in charge of the big *and* little things in my life. Once I started to look at things differently, my reaction to things changed. When I had an excruciating headache or tears appeared out of nowhere, I tried to remember God had a reason for this event. It didn't make things resolve more quickly, but I was able to accept that this was God's plan.

*Therefore we do not lose heart. Though outwardly we are wasting away, yet inwardly we are being renewed day by day.*

*2 Corinthians 4:16*

This was one of the many verses that I repeated throughout the long days. It is God's promise that day by day, we will be renewed. It is our responsibility to not lose heart.

Tying your shoes doesn't mean there won't be tears; it doesn't mean there won't be difficult times. It just means that you have faith and trust God that this is his plan, and he will never leave your side.

From the moment my husband died, I knew that this was his plan. While my faith sometimes wavered, God never left my side, and his promises never changed. Even when my faith and trust in God felt strong, there have been many days I've spent just tying my shoes. I have shed more tears in the year after my husband died than I have in my entire lifetime, and there have been many difficult times. But even through the pain, I knew that it was okay, because God had a plan. A plan to prosper me and not to harm me.

*"For I know the plans I have for you," declares*
*the Lord. "Plans to prosper you and not harm you.*
*Plans to give you hope and a future."*

*Jeremiah 29:11*

God is amazing. He gives us what he knows that we need, when we need it. From the beginning I wanted more strength, but God knew that I had what I needed at the time. It was in May, almost ten months after my husband had died, that I realized that not only was God giving me strength to accept the twists and turns of the roller coaster, but he was giving me the courage to be at the edge of the emotional cliff and fall off. And then get back up. I learned that even though it's hard, God will always give me the strength and courage to get back up and keep going.

I must stay ready and open for anything God has for me.

# CHAPTER 8

# You Can Lead a Horse to Water, But You Can't Stop Your Emotions

*emotions*

Those who sow with tears will reap with songs of joy.

Psalm 126:5

You may have heard the saying "You can lead a horse to water, but you can't make him drink." This is true. In grief one could also say "You can lead a horse to water, but you can't stop your emotions." This is also very true. You can delay your emotions. You can try and ignore your emotions. But unless you face your emotions, they will never go away. In fact, they will come back again and again, and with a vengeance.

As I have said before, from the beginning I knew Dave's death was part of God's plan. I knew. But it doesn't mean that I wasn't sad, and it certainly doesn't mean that I did not cry. I have cried just about everywhere. In my house, on my patio, in my car, in restaurants, grocery stores, the doctor's office, and the chiropractor's office, at friends' houses, at church, in hotels, in airports, in my office, in classrooms, in hallways, in bathrooms. Just about everywhere. I never knew that I had so many tears. But God knows everything.

*Record my lament; list my tears on your scroll—*
*are they not in your record?*

Psalm 56:8

There were times that I did not want to shed those tears. Usually this happened when I was around other people that were not part of my "safety net." So I found ways to push back the wall of emotions. I learned to bite my lip or fingernails to try to ward off tears. When I wanted to be less obvious of my struggle at the moment, I would bite the side of my tongue. This was effective until I realized that I was getting painful sores from biting down so hard. I was able to end that bad habit very quickly.

To keep my emotions at bay, I also learned to disengage myself from what was happening. There were times I would be in the middle of a meeting and memories would arrive like a flood. If I stared straight ahead, or pretended to take notes, I could usually get through the moment. I'm sure I missed some important pieces of information this way, but at the time, survival without tears was the only thing on my mind. I've often wondered if people noticed my non-attention at these times. I know at least a few were able to perceive what was happening. They were also kind enough to not call me on it at that particular moment.

Emotions are heavy. I have spent enough time holding emotions back to have learned that. I also have learned that for every time you keep your emotions contained, they will express themselves with much more intensity the next time. They become heavier.

Emotions are also exhausting. Countless times I wrote in my journal that I was exhausted. And that doesn't include all the times I didn't write in my journal because I was too tired! At some point,

I stopped writing down that I was tired, because it had just become part of my life.

## When Do the Tears End?

After their dad died, Stacey and Kristen had stayed at home until August 4 for a reason. They wanted to be there for me on August 3, the day that would have been our twenty-ninth wedding anniversary. When I realized the reasoning of their departure date, my heart was filled with an overwhelming love for them. I took them both to the airport so they could return to their respective homes. I gave them each a hug and a kiss and said good-bye. Then I walked out of the airport with tears in my eyes. I felt another change occurring. Even though I felt like I was all by myself at that moment, God made it very clear to me that I was never once by myself. He had always been right by my side. I just didn't always see clearly.

That God was near became clear anytime anyone sat and listened to me. In fact, in my grief, the best thing anyone ever did for me was to listen. My emotions were on such a roller coaster that I often didn't know which way was up. But usually if someone gave me the opportunity, I was able to articulate something. If they were only willing to wait and listen. And when that happened I felt like the most important person in the world.

But still, it was hard to explain my emotions. Confusion was so much a part of my life. It was hard to explain my thoughts and feelings to others. I couldn't say these words to anyone, so it became very important for me to write them down. I was trying to figure out what my new life was supposed to be. How to rebuild my life.

My co-worker Linda is one of the most perceptive people I have ever met. She always knew how I felt just by looking at me. I could never fool her, so at some point I stopped trying and answered honestly. She listened and understood when I told her that everything felt so different, that I felt like I was living someone else's life. Now I know that this is my life. It just looks and feels very different. I'm getting used to it, but I will never forget my old life.

Someone once asked me, "When do the tears end?" I said I didn't think that they ever do end. Even a year after Dave died, I still have tears. They are not as uncontrollable as in the past, but they are there. So I do not know when the tears end. If that ever happens, I'll let you know. More likely than not I was correct with my initial response—they never do end.

## The Hardness of Grief

Grieving is much harder than I thought. If you really choose to go through grief, and not around it, grief is exhausting and painful. But it is well worth it. I now allow myself the luxury of revisiting memories and the details, and even though there are sometimes tears, it's okay. The joy that I receive from remembering the good things is awesome.

I only went to one funeral in the months after Dave died, but I went to several visitations. With each visitation or funeral I attended, I relived my own experiences of when Dave died. I was torn, because I wanted to be there for the family, but I also didn't want to fall apart. I had never been in a funeral home so many times in such a short period of time, and it still makes me wonder why God chose to have those events occur in my life at that time. I hope to find out someday.

As I have said, everything affected me and almost anything could bring me to tears. I have accepted that there will be emotions when I least expect it, but I am still guarded as to when I will allow myself to express these emotions in front of others. And I can definitely think of Dave now without dissolving into a puddle of tears. Sometimes there are small streams or mini-puddles, but that's progress. Baby steps.

Most times I would have preferred if people automatically knew how I was feeling. That would have been so much easier. While it did help me to talk about Dave's death, I was always concerned that people would get tired of listening to me. Sometimes just knowing that people knew that I was grieving was helpful. I wanted people to know that my feelings at that time were rather unstable, and that they would need to be patient with me. Eventually with time things improved, and I am so thankful for those people that were, and still are, patient with me.

## Worry

One day, on my way to see a student, I almost got hit by a van pulling out of a driveway. I swerved to avoid getting hit or the results would not have been good.

When this happened, I shared this with only a few people. That is how much that it scared me. This memory is as vivid as the day that it happened. The only difference is that I don't feel the sheer panic I experienced at that time. I am so thankful for that.

I still have "what if" fears. *What if something happens to me?* I worry when people I care about travel. *What if their plane/car/bus is in an accident?* I worry when people are experiencing health problems. *What if the doctors can't fix what is wrong? What is God's plan and what if I don't like it?*

I play the "what if" game way too often, especially at night. It takes a lot of prayer to push those fears aside and focus on God. And if I don't like God's plan, it doesn't matter because I really don't have a choice in the matter. But I do know that he will always give me the strength I need to face any battle. I am ready.

The November after Dave died, I wrote in my journal:

> *Sometimes I just don't know. Here are some words I've thought of to describe how I feel*

* *tired*
* *confused*
* *overwhelmed*
* *anxious*
* *scared*
* *lacking confidence*
* *sad*
* *2 steps forward, 1 step back*
* *content—only sometimes, but I know God wants me to be content in all circumstances*

The funny thing is, many of those words still describe my feelings today. Except that I have a few words to add to the list:

* stronger
* blessed
* calm—not always, but prayer and taking deep breaths helps immensely with this
* hopeful
* loved

I would have added something else, but I couldn't think of the word to describe the fact that sometimes I am happy and I smile. I even laugh. Only God could have performed that miracle.

Even with this, sometimes I feel like by being content or being busy or being okay with this new chapter in my life, it means that I'm forgetting Dave, or I don't care, or that I didn't love him.

I love my husband. I always have and always will. I now understand and believe that it is good to move forward with my life. It doesn't mean that I am forgetting the man that I married. He will forever be my always.

*Blessed is the man who perseveres under trial, because*
*when he has stood the test, he will receive the crown of life*
*that God has promised to those who love him.*

*James 1:12*

It is said that grief lasts at least one year. That gives the person left behind the opportunity to face all of the "firsts": first Christmas without your loved one, first Thanksgiving, etc. But they also say that two years of grief is actually more accurate. In fact, it is not at all unusual for grief to last much longer than that. Even forever. And that makes sense, because how do you recover from having your heart ripped out and your life torn to pieces? It's not easy, but with God anything is possible. Even if grief lasts for the rest of your life.

*Cast your cares on the Lord and He will sustain you; He*
*will never let the righteous fall.*

*Psalm 55:22*

In December, I was still working with insurance companies with issues related to Dave's hospitalization and death. With each form that I filled out and delivered and each phone call that I made, I was reminded of why I was completing these tasks. Why I was on this path. My husband was no longer on this Earth. Emotions were present during each one of these experiences. God was with me at these times, even when I didn't consciously call on his name. He was just there. No matter what. I am now finished dealing with insurance companies, but there are other things that need to be done. Whatever happens I know that I will not be alone.

*Lord I wait for you; you will answer, Lord my God.*

*Psalm 38:15*

## A New Stage

Early in the New Year I found myself very emotional. Tears again came when I least expected them. It felt like I was moving to a different stage of grief. Grief has many stages, although it is not linear. One does not cleanly go through Step One, then Step Two, etc. It is more like moving back and forth. Sometimes it's hard to tell where you are. Early in the year, I really did feel like I was in a different stage of grief. I was much more aware of what was going on in life, and much more aware of my feelings. I felt as though I was beginning to understand things and gain some control. Even though moving to a new stage of grief was a good thing, it was also scary because it meant something different. A change.

That was around the same time God lifted off that layer of the blindfold. I could see better, but I started to get scared. In the past, I had been going through life depending on others to help get me through the day. But now I could see and felt like I should be able to get through the day on my own. I was wrong about that. I should have turned to God, but I didn't always remember to do that. God has given me lots of opportunities to practice turning to him, and I have gotten better at this. But I still need to improve.

During this time, a friend told me that when she thinks of two certain women, she thinks of the word *grace*. She said that I am one of those women.

I was speechless and confused when I heard these words. I didn't understand how the word *grace* could be used to describe me. Especially when this friend had seen me cry and fall apart numerous times at the smallest little thing. But I accepted the compliment. Later as I thought about this, I realized it is not what you say or if you can control your emotions in certain situations, but how you live your life that makes the biggest impact on people. The big picture.

Grief is messy, exhausting, and confusing. I don't think I was making it any harder than it really was, but at the time I wasn't sure. It took me a long time to become comfortable with my feelings. It took even longer to admit to others what those emotions were. I wish I had faced my emotions sooner.

The March after Dave died, Kristen and I went to Disney World. In a way, going on vacation was a leap of faith. I had been to Disney three times before this, so I had a general idea of what to expect. But this time I would be doing all this without my husband.

While at Disney I definitely had memories, but they did not immobilize me as I had feared. They were just memories of what a good time I had in the past. This Disney vacation was different than the others. I now have new memories to treasure, but I will never forget the memories of going to Disney with my husband.

But the trip stirred up more than just memories. It also stirred up anxiety. Travel is frustrating. Especially when you are tired, and the person you are traveling with is very tired. During the flight from Green Bay to Detroit I had so many fears/anxieties:

> *What if I forgot something?*
> *What if this is too stressful?*
> *What if I don't have any time to myself?*
> *What if the entire spring break passes me by?*
> *What if I have fun without Dave?*
> *What if?*

I realized that not only was this the first big vacation without Dave, it was also the first big vacation that I've taken by myself—ever. I wasn't sure what to do with that.

Obviously, even something fun could wreak havoc in my life. I tried not to show it because I didn't think anyone would understand. I mean, who wouldn't be excited about going to a warm and sunny place like Florida? But the emotions that these fears stirred in me were very real. In the end this is what happened:

*\* I didn't forget anything—and if I had I'm sure that I could have bought a replacement.*

*\* Vacation always causes stress, and this one was no exception. But the stress was not overwhelming.*

*\* I had time by myself—even if there were people around me. I have gotten very good at being in my own world even when around others.*

*\* We arrived home late Thursday evening, which meant I still had a few days of my spring break left.*

*\* I had fun without Dave, and I survived. I know he would have wanted me to have a good time, and I did. I met almost every princess in the park and enjoyed myself while doing it.*

So although my fears were very real to me at the time, I really didn't have to worry about anything. But if you had tried to tell me that before I left on vacation, I might have told you that you were crazy. I wish I could say that I have not played the "what if" game since that time. But I would be lying if I said that. At least now when I start to do that I remember to talk to God and ask him to calm my fears. Sometimes.

## Naming My Emotions

I always figured that if I could name my emotions then I could deal with them. But there were times that I wasn't sure what I was feeling, and that made things difficult. If I had to put a name to what I was feeling at the time, I would say fear. Fear of the unknown. When faced with the unknown God wants us to trust him. Easier said than done.

The problem was that I didn't like the place where I was then. It wasn't comfortable. In all the months since Dave died, I had always known that God was there, and I felt his presence. But for a short time, I experienced not feeling or hearing God for a few days. Very long days. I panicked because of what I couldn't hear or feel. It scared me because I was so unsure of what was happening. As I think back, I understand that God was there, just in a different way. He was letting me experience my life without the ability to hear or feel him. I like to think that God was giving me a faith checkup. In my eyes I failed miserably. But I learned a very valuable lesson: even if I can't hear or feel God, he is right there next to me. I just need to have faith. It's okay if he is quiet for a while. He must be trying to teach me something.

*For we walk by faith, not by sight.*

*2 Corinthians 5:7*

### Firsts

People think about the big things—all the "big firsts" (first Christmas, etc.) when someone dies. No one ever talks about all the "little firsts." I think those are harder because people don't acknowledge them. Some of them have been tough. Little firsts, like first walk, first time grocery shopping, first vacation, first taxes, first time you have really good news, first time something doesn't go right at work, first time at church. Actually, maybe it's everything.

There are so many little firsts that it would be impossible to name them all. And I'm sure that it's different for everyone. But I do think that the little firsts have been harder.

With all the little firsts, I began to think about how to measure and describe my emotions. I finally came up with this: I measure them in "Steps from a Cliff." As in, *How many steps am I away from the edge of the cliff before I fall off and fall apart?* Of course, the answer varies throughout the day. A lot.

I don't know how or why I came up with this, but it happened. How many steps am I away from the cliff? Often it was only one or two steps. Sometimes I was so close to the edge that I knew that if someone breathed on me I would fall off. And there were times that I did fall off the cliff—especially as grief intensified at three and nine months. But God was always there to catch me.

When I felt myself nearing the edge of the cliff, I'd reach out to someone. Before I reached the edge of the cliff and went sliding down the mountain, I would call a friend. We would talk and talk, and after a while I could feel myself moving away from the edge. I am so thankful for friends that I can call at any time of the day or night. Friends that will listen as I talk, and friends that will talk to me when all I can do is cry.

> *It is God who arms me with strength and keeps*
> *my way secure.*
>
> Psalm 18:32

## The Meaning of Things

The spring after Dave died, I wrote in my journal: *I think I am feeling joy. Or happiness. Whichever one is momentary. I'm not sure. But overall I am content.*

I had asked several people about joy. What is it? What does it feel like? And what is the difference between joy and happiness? I received varying answers, so I am still not sure as to whether I was feeling joy or happiness at that moment. But it really doesn't matter. I just knew that it was something different than sadness.

Someone once told me that strength meant continuing to get up when you're knocked down and faced with difficult situations. That made sense to me. And sometimes, expressing those emotions and crying those tears in front of others takes more strength and courage than you would ever imagine—and can lead to joy. Or happiness.

I have felt so many different emotions since Dave died, and I often wanted to understand what emotion I was feeling. Calmness was always a welcome change from feeling overwhelmed and anxious. It took a lot of faith in God to even believe that feeling anything besides sadness was a possibility, and it is crucial that I keep my eyes on him. For it is when we turn away from God that we start to doubt.

> *He replied, "If you have faith as small as mustard seed,*
> *you can say to this mulberry tree, 'Be uprooted and*
> *planted in the sea'; and it will obey you."*
>
> *Luke 17:6*

So many songs bring back memories and have a special place in my heart. Many of those songs I listen to every day in my car, but often when I hear those songs in a different environment, they touch my heart, and I end up in tears. Emotions are that unpredictable.

I have cried a lot of tears. A lot. But I didn't always admit the reason why. There were many times I used the excuse that I was tired, or overwhelmed at work. And I'm sure I did feel that way, but I think there were also times that I just wasn't honest with myself and others. There are times now that I cry for other reasons (it's the truth), but there are some times that my tears are simply because my best friend died. Being able to be honest about this hasn't changed my circumstances, but it has been a step forward.

Many other things have helped me step forward as well. For example, I had worked on a slideshow of pictures of Dave and our family for months and was excited about it. But when I finished it I was sad, because I knew it was another part of my life that was over; something else that I had to let go of. I still watch that slideshow and think about all the good times that we had. Sometimes I get sad when I take that walk down memory lane, but I am also reminded that I will see my husband again in Heaven someday. I look forward to that day.

Even though my husband and best friend died, I can say that good things have happened. I realize that I have been blessed more than I thought possible. All along God knew what he was doing and had a plan. I don't always understand what happens, but I do know that when I am having a rough day I have some very supportive people around me to remind me that there is a purpose in all of this.

That said, it's still hard to understand. At first, seeing couples together or hearing about anniversaries did not bother me. But over time, I became very aware of those things. I can recall times that my husband talked about how we would celebrate our thirtieth anniversary. His most recent idea had been to take a cruise. His life ended and we will never be able to enjoy that cruise, and for that reason I am sad. However I am able to rejoice, because I know that he is in Heaven now, and I'm sure that is better than any cruise that he ever could have imagined.

July—the year after Dave died—was an emotional month. Not only was I able to recognize that it was difficult for me, but I was also able to consider that it might be hard for others. There were so many times over the past months that I wanted to yell at God and tell him to stop the storms, to make everything peaceful again. And even though I did have those conversations with God, I knew that he was with me during the storms. He was there at night when things often seemed the darkest, and he was there during the day when the rain poured down. He will be there with me everyday no matter what the weather—or my attitude—is like.

## Changing Emotions

The day Dave died truly was one of the most unbelievable days. On that day Dave was supposed to go home, to our house in Green Bay. Instead he went home to Heaven. I will never forget having to tell people that the man that they thought was improving in health had instead died and gone to Heaven. I will never forget the emotion that I heard in their voices and saw in their faces. I will also never forget the love and support that they provided to me.

Likewise, the one-year anniversary of his death was exhausting and emotional. It was also a day that I will never forget. I will never forget that I was able to share with people what Dave meant to me, and I will never forget that I will someday be able to see him again in Heaven. I will never forget.

> *Your love, O Lord, reaches to the heavens, Your faithfulness to the skies.*
>
> *Psalm 36:5*

# CHAPTER 9

# WHAT'S GOOD FOR THE GOOSE ISN'T ALWAYS GOOD FOR THE GANDER

*decide what's right for you*

*Above all else guard your heart, for everything you do flows from it.*

*Proverbs 4:23*

When someone dies, people want to help the person left behind. One way to help is to make suggestions. This is not a bad thing to do. However, not everything works for every person. So it is important to decide for yourself if something is right for you. One of the best ways to achieve this is through prayer and by surrounding yourself with godly people who have values that are similar to yours.

I listened when others made suggestions. I thought about their reasoning on things. Sometimes I took their advice; sometimes I did not. There were times I made choices and decisions all by myself (even though it often took a long time to finally decide).

The September after Dave died, I started to think about Christmas. I knew this holiday would be very different without my husband by my side. I wondered if it would really make that much of a difference to people that Dave was gone. Would they remember him? I knew they would, but grief does funny things to you. It can cause you to lose perspective on the truth. So it was out of desperation that I began thinking of ways to make sure that Dave was not forgotten at Christmas. It was out of desperation that I embarked on a race to find the perfect Christmas ornament to give to family and friends.

I chose an ornament because it was Christmas and it made sense. I knew everyone would take out those ornaments each year, and they would be reminded of a great man. After searching online, I finally chose several different items. The young nieces and nephews would receive a stuffed Packers snowman ornament. Others would receive a football-shaped ornament with the Green Bay Packers logo. Each ornament was adorned with a wooden gift tag that read "Love Uncle Dave," "Love, Dave," or 'I Love You!!! Dave." The words on the tags were in Dave's own handwriting and were taken from cards or letters that he had sent. They were beautiful.

One special ornament was given to only one person. I gave a small replica of a Packers baseball hat (the exact kind that Dave used to wear to work on a daily basis) to Dave's friend and co-worker.

I felt good about these ornaments and looked forward to sharing them with family and friends. I don't think I really thought about how people would react when they opened these special gifts, and therefore I was not prepared for their responses. Some people expressed themselves with tears; others were speechless. But the most heartfelt response came from Dave's best friend, Jay.

Shortly after Christmas Jay and his wife moved to a new house. They shared with me that on their moving day Dave's ornament and picture were the first things to be unpacked, and they were given a special place of honor in their new home. This one small action confirmed in my heart that all my apprehensions were wrong. Dave would never be forgotten. Giving those ornaments to others that Christmas was the right thing for me to do. It might not work for someone else.

There are some choices that I made very quickly. I love music, and so did Dave. Whenever we got in the car the radio was playing. Because we both liked music, I asked Kristen to make some CDs for me that included songs that were important to me. One CD had songs that had special meaning to me, and the other CD had songs that Dave liked. While I wanted to be able to hear songs that Dave had enjoyed, I made the conscious decision to include only songs that I also liked.

I have listened to those CDs many times—so often I have wondered if they would wear out. And I know asking Kristen to make those CDs was one of the best choices that I have made. Listening to this music gives me comfort and security in a world that feels like it is spinning upside down. It may not be what someone else would choose to do, but it works for me.

In the weeks after Dave died I purposely scheduled appointments mid-morning. This assured me that I would get up in the morning and get out of the house. I also planned activities on the weekends to make sure that my days were busy. Once I went back to work I didn't have to worry about any of that. My days were scheduled for me.

Because grief sucks all the energy out of you (it seems as though it takes twice as much energy to do a fraction of the work that you used to do!), on the days I didn't accomplish much, I tried to be okay with it. In the beginning it didn't take much convincing, but as the months progressed I always felt like I should do more. Sometimes I even tried to do more, but I was never very successful. Whatever I did, whether it was going to a movie or out to dinner with friends, it always left me exhausted. But it was important to me to stay involved in life and not spend my days just sitting on the couch and watching TV.

Again, however, what worked for me doesn't work for everyone.

After the death of a loved one some people return to work right away. Because of the school calendar I was able to be away from work for a full month. Regardless of this time frame, work was difficult. And being tired, which I experienced on a daily basis, did make things more challenging. While some people suggested that I could take a leave of absence, I chose to stay at work and use sick days as needed. I chose to do this because it was right for me. Someone else may have chosen a different path.

I heard more about the different paths of grief people experienced at my GriefShare meetings. When I first heard about these support groups for people who have experienced the death of a loved one, I knew I wanted to attend, but I really did not know what to expect. Meetings were held every Monday night at my church. Although they were sometimes difficult, I started to look forward to Monday nights. I was even disappointed when I was unable to attend. The best part of these meetings is that I met others who had begun this journey before I had. Others who could describe what it had been like for them.

In reality I knew that the best way to heal was to talk about what I was experiencing. However on some evenings at GriefShare, perhaps because I did not want to appear weak in front of the others, I didn't share much. While this helped me to not cry, it didn't help me to move forward in my grief. I have since accepted that I need to be honest about my feelings, which sometimes means that I need to cry in front of other people. Even if I don't like it. In the end I usually feel just a little bit better.

## Making Changes

I made several other changes to help with grieving, including sleeping under a weighted blanket (not everyone likes them, but sinking to sleep under one worked for me!) I even tried sleeping on the other side of the bed. Usually I sleep on the left side of the bed. One night, for whatever reason, I slept on the right side. I don't know why. For something different? So the mattress didn't get uneven? At the time I thought it would be a good idea. But I had trouble getting to sleep. And I didn't sleep for very long. Finally at midnight I moved things around and went back to the left side of the bed. It felt comfortable and familiar.

I was surprised at what a difference it made to try and sleep on the other side of the bed. Maybe I thought that I would feel closer to my husband if I slept on his side of the bed, but that didn't work. Comfortable and familiar. That's what works for me.

But I did switch which days I shopped on. Dave and I always went "big shopping" on Friday night. Shopping without my husband was different. I found when I shopped on Fridays, I missed having him by my side, pushing the cart, and trying to sneak Hershey bars and anything else into the cart. I found that shopping on a Saturday morning was a better choice for me.

**Processing Emotions**

I recognize that there is a definite progression of how I face things when something is bothering me:

1. I think about it
2. I write about it
3. I think about it more and say it out loud to myself
4. I say it out loud to someone else

I need to get to the last step in order to try and accept it. Sometimes there is a long time between steps.

Everyone faces things differently. While traveling through the grief journey, it has been critical for me to look closely at each aspect of my life—and that includes myself. Understanding yourself helps you to rebuild your life.

I started writing in my journal after my husband died, and it has helped me in several ways. First of all, it has helped me to remember what has happened (difficulty remembering things—a side effect of grief) in my day-to-day life. It has also given me the opportunity to look back and see that I have traveled forward. In August, I had difficulty choosing what socks to wear, but several months later I had the ability to plan a vacation.

There have been some things that I have thought about, but have never written. There are just some things that I will probably never write. But that's okay, because God knows my heart. I would highly recommend writing in a journal. But if you choose not to, that's okay. Writing is not for everyone. Find something that works for you.

Even though I write, I have a tendency to remember things in pictures. This is helpful when trying to think of where something is located in the house. I picture it, and can see that it is on the top shelf in the corner cabinet behind the glassware. Since Dave died this has not really changed. When I look at old CDs, I can see us riding in his car listening to the music. When I think of certain foods, I see myself cooking dinner and then the two of us sitting down to a nice meal together. There are just some things that I think of as "Dave things" and even now have difficulty facing. Which I guess is why I don't listen to the old CDs or watch his favorite movies very often. And when I do cook, I often prepare different foods than what we used to eat together. And that's okay.

When someone dies, one of the things that needs to be done is going through closets and drawers. So as summer break began, I told myself that was one of the things that I wanted to accomplish. I started cleaning closets, but quickly had more questions than I started with. I was able to get rid of a few things, but there were some things that just held too many memories, like the salt-and-pepper shaker that we never used but had held memories for Dave. And that is why it is still in my cupboard, taking up very little physical space but a big part of my heart. Luckily, grief has no timetable and there is no due date of when all this cleaning needs to be completed. I figure if I'm having difficulty getting rid of a salt-and-pepper shaker, then maybe I'm not ready to let go of some of the bigger things.

## Things to Do

When Dave was alive, I never concerned myself over finding things to do. The school year was busy enough, and during the summer, if we went for a walk after supper or sat at home and watched a movie, I was fine with that. The important part was that we were together. These days I find that it is important to keep busy, but God also tells us to be still. Finding the balance between the two is both important and difficult.

After Dave died I often felt like I needed to be busy. Even during the school year, I needed something to focus on to help me to feel that I was doing something important. I made Christmas ornaments, slideshow/videos, and wrote in my journal. A few weeks after my husband died, I decided that I wanted to make a scrapbook, but never really had a good picture in my mind of what it would look like. I also wanted it to be perfect and didn't want to risk making a mistake. When I finally decided to work on the album it came together quickly. I have a variety of mementos and photographs in the scrapbook. I don't know if it's perfect, but it says what I want it to say. That I love my husband with all my heart. He will forever be my always.

I wasn't sure what I would do on the anniversary of Dave's death. At first I thought about staying home and spending the day by myself, just as I had done the previous year. But ideas change, and I'm glad that they did. On that day I went to the chiropractor, had lunch with Dave's sister, and went to dinner with a friend. I even had time for a much needed nap that afternoon. Spending the day with people helped me to keep busy, but I also was able to spend time with my memories. For me, it was a good day. The only thing that would have made the day better was if I could have shared it with my husband.

> *Commit to the Lord whatever you do, and your plans will succeed.*
>
> *Proverbs 16:3*

# CHAPTER 10

# BE LIKE ISAAC

*confidence*

*But blessed is the man who trusts in the Lord,*
*whose confidence is in Him.*

*Jeremiah 17:7*

In November 2014 I had the absolute pleasure and honor to begin working with a young man named Isaac. He was four years old at the time.

When I first met Isaac he was filled with apprehension and uncertainty. And manners. At the beginning of the school year, he had conquered the difficult task of walking to the classroom with the rest of the group. As I watched Isaac in the classroom with his four-year-old friends, I noticed that he was very quiet. In general he followed along with the group, but when asked to participate in specific activities, such as playing Head, Shoulders, Knees and Toes, he would calmly look at the speaker, smile, and say, "No thank you." How could anyone resist such a polite, honest answer? I knew that there was a lot that I could learn from Isaac.

As the months progressed, Isaac and I practiced many different skills away from his peers. This gave him a chance to try new things without the pressure of others waiting for him or expecting too much. He attempted everything that I asked of him and more. Isaac flourished.

One day I asked Isaac to complete a relatively new and difficult task. He smiled and looked up at me with sparkling eyes and said, "I can do that!"

Isaac had become confident and was willing to take risks. I will never forget that moment.

I wish I could say that I have always been like Isaac. I hope to get there someday. For now my confidence level is still weak and seems to change as often as the weather. Many times I have talked to God about these feelings, and he reminds me of what I already know. These are some of those debates I have had with God. Guess who won each time?

> *Me: I'm so tired. How am I going to make it through this week?*
>
> *God: Do not worry about tomorrow.*
>
> *Me: Well, how am I going to make it through today? I can't.*
>
> *God: You can't by yourself. But together we can.*
>
> *Me: But....*
>
> *God: You will. Trust me.*

And when it came to writing these words I had another discussion with God.

> *Me: Are you sure you want me to write this?*
>
> *God: Yes. You.*
>
> *Me: But I can't write.*
>
> *God: I will give you the words.*
>
> *Me: Who would ever want to read something that I wrote?*

*God: Remember, it is I that will be giving you the words to write.*

*Me: But what if no one reads it?*

*God: Does it matter?*

*Me: Well, no.*

I think you get the picture. It has been difficult at times to remember that God is in control. Recently I added another conversation with God. This one has taken place many times.

*Me: God, I am putting my heart and soul into writing these words. What if no one reads it?*

*God: Does it matter?*

*Me: Well, no. But God, I am putting my heart and soul into writing these words. What if someone reads it?????*

*God: When someone reads these words they will hear what they need to hear.*

*Me: Okay. I trust you God.*

It may not make sense, but that is what those conversations with God sounded like. Luckily I had enough confidence and faith to believe that God was in control and that he knew what he was doing. But it doesn't mean that I didn't question things.

In the days before Dave died, I had been confident that Dave was going to improve. I knew he would be coming home with me. Just hearing the message from the doctor that he had 'taken a turn for the worse' brought fear to my mind. When I talked to the doctor, he told me that although my husband's condition had worsened, he was out of the woods. I felt kind of bad because I had panicked instead of trusting God.

Then, on the day he died, I was absolutely positive that medical emergency alarms at the hospital had nothing to do with my husband. I was confident it would only be a few more minutes until the nurse came and told me that my husband was ready for a visitor. That didn't happen. I think that is the moment when my confidence began to waver.

## Trusting and Believing

Right away Stacey told me that she wanted to speak at Dave's funeral. At first I questioned her because I thought it would be too difficult. But I know my daughter, and I know that she is very good at speaking in front of groups. Public speaking does not appeal to me. To me, any group that is larger than three adults is too much for me. However, on Saturday morning, two days after his death, I woke up and I knew what God wanted me to do. So without a doubt in my mind I started listening to God and preparing what I would say on the day of my husband's funeral.

The funeral was Monday morning. God spoke through me. I know because I have never talked in front of that many people, and yet I felt completely at peace about it. As I stood up in church at my husband's funeral, I was calm. Only God could have performed that miracle. When I think back to that day it's still hard to believe that I spoke in front of all those people.

Even still there have been many days that I have struggled. But I never questioned God's love for me. I am so thankful that God is patient with me and that he will not give up on me. Even when I go to him with the same questions and insecurities over and over.

This feeling of "I can't do this" did not occur everyday. However, when it does happen and I remember that God is by my side giving me strength, then I am able to answer instead: "I can do that." It may not be with the confidence of Isaac, but I am learning.

So for instance, when Kristen's car died, I realized this was the first crisis that I had to face without my husband and I thought, "I can't do this." Dave had always taken care of car issues, but it was no longer an option to hand the phone over to him. Instead I had to turn to God, and trust God to tell me what I should do. To me, that was the only choice that made any sense.

*When I am afraid, I will trust in you.*

*Psalm 56:3*

At the end of the day, I tried to say, "I did it." I always tried to look for the good in anything. Sometimes I had to look hard and really reach to find the positive side of things. There were also times that I was able to smile and think "I did it!" But in reality I never did these things on my own—God was always there to help me.

I cannot imagine being on this journey without God. He has brought me through so much, and I know he will be with me forever. It hasn't been easy and it hasn't been fun. But I am confident that this is what God wants me to experience right now.

In fact, when a friend asked me why Dave died (not *how*, but *why*), I answered in the only way I knew how: it was God's plan. God had a better idea. I am still confident of this.

While I have always been confident that Dave's death was part of God's plan, there have been other things in my life that I wasn't so sure of. One particular day, I came face to face with the reality that this grief journey was going to be more than I had expected. There is one thing that I am sure of now, and it is the fact that grief is extremely hard.

One GriefShare message we heard said grief lasts longer than you would ever imagine. It is true. Grief lasts a long time. The good news is that now I understand and accept this as part of my life. But I try not to let it run my life. I am learning.

## Prayer

The fall after Dave died, I wrote in my journal: *I chose to do the thing that I believe God wants me to do . . . I don't have a lot of confidence now, so I'm praying for that also.*

I always believed God wanted me to work during the school year. Sometimes I had to dig down deep to remember this, but when I got past all the fears and exhaustion, I always came to the same conclusion. There were numerous times I felt like I couldn't work another day. But I also knew that God would always give me the strength that I needed for that day. Not only that, but he provided friends I could talk to about my uncertainties. It has been far from easy, but I know it is what God wanted me to do.

Though sometimes I forgot that God was with me. I didn't mean to, but during those moments of uncertainty I would forget. The good news is that the more I turned to God, the more I remembered him when things became difficult.

I have always known that I needed to go through grief instead of avoiding it. I am so thankful that even when it was hard to pray, God was still there watching over me and protecting me.

Every day I asked God for strength, and every day God gave me exactly what I needed. There were many days that I wished for more, and many days I wished that I didn't have to experience this grief journey. But in the end I am confident that God knows what he is doing, even if it doesn't make sense right now.

*Lord, you are my God; I will exalt you and praise your name, for in perfect faithfulness you have done wonderful things, things planned long ago.*

*Isaiah 25:1*

It took me many months before I was willing to admit to others that things were not okay. Even though I knew God was always there with me, sometimes I needed a person to talk to and a shoulder to cry on. God provided that for me and blessed me with friends that have been there for me no matter what. Or when.

There were many times during the school year that I felt like I was not completing my job as well as I could. I had co-workers who assured me I was wrong, but I still had times I questioned myself. It was an exciting day when I realized that I did know what I was doing, and I was doing the best that I was able to at the moment.

Sometimes the storms in my life seemed to continue forever. And while I knew that God was in control, there were times that this was difficult to remember. There were times that I felt so alone, but I knew that this was never true.

There is one thing that I have always known, and that is that God wants me to turn to him. He delights in it. The more I ask God for strength, the more he provides.

## Finding Strength

In the months after Dave died, I didn't watch a lot of TV. I often had it on, but more for background noise. For many months I really only watched three different shows. Two were sitcoms and one was a reality show. I was able to watch the sitcoms because I had seen them so many times that I knew the story. I could see one scene and know what was going to happen. The same thing always happened. It never changed and I liked that. I was able to watch the reality show because it was one that Dave and I had always watched together. It was a "popcorn show." It also felt comfortable because it was something in my life that was the same. Sort of.

These were times that helped me feel confident. Just like Isaac. But then I would face another situation just hours or a day later, and I would be so unsure of myself. My ability to believe in myself and my skills seemed to vary as much as the tide. There were times that it was difficult to pray, so I am thankful that there were others that took care of that when I was unable to do so.

I know my life will continue to change, but the memories will stay the same. God will stay the same.

*But you remain the same, and your years will never end.*

*Psalm 102:27*

By springtime, I had started to enjoy going on walks again, and God often used these times to speak to me. I was not very excited when I heard God telling me to stop procrastinating and stop avoiding the difficult things in life. But I understood. These are the things that God uses to teach. I was confident that God was telling me this for a reason.

With everything that happened in the nine months after Dave died, the thing that I felt most secure about and the most at peace about was that Dave is in Heaven. I know that for a fact and I accept that. I am still sad that he is not here and I miss him—sometimes so much that it hurts. But I know that he is no longer in pain.

Sometimes it seemed that the only thing that did make sense was that my husband was in Heaven. I was confident of this. I also knew that in all of this, he was the lucky one. Dave is the one walking on the streets of gold now.

Whatever "first" tasks lie before me or whatever grief I endure, whenever I lack confidence, I remind myself: "Yes, I can do this." God is changing my life into what he wants it to be.

Through all the pain and the turmoil, God has taught me that there is a lot I can do. It may not be easy, but if it is something that is in his plan, then I can accomplish it. I just need to keep my eyes fully focused on him.

So when an administrator gently told my colleagues and I that we were moving to a new office at the end of the school year, I didn't cry, as I'd wanted to back in September. By May, I was ready to hear the news and think, *It's okay. I can do this.* God has done a lot of work in my life.

God certainly has done a lot in my life since my husband died. He has helped me to find the strength that I never knew I possessed. He has helped me understand that life can continue without your best friend by your side. But most importantly of all, he has shown me that he will be by my side at all times, no matter what. So when I heard that we were moving to a new office, I saw it as an opportunity to have faith and trust that God knows what is best. After all, God has much better ideas than I could ever think of.

When we first saw our new office, my office-mates and I immediately noticed how cozy it was (it was smaller than our previous office). In the end, I felt good about this change. Somehow I knew that God had a purpose for this change, even if it didn't seem right at the time.

It wasn't unlike the day I noticed a little flower in my garden filled with weeds. I didn't plant it. It just grew. I know this was a God-thing.

Every spring Dave went out and bought a variety of flowers and planted them in front of the house. That was something he liked to do. Gardening is not my favorite task, so I chose not to plant any flowers in the spring. I ended up with a garden full of weeds, which I occasionally pulled. But on that day I noticed a flower among all the weeds, and I knew it was from my husband. I knew he was telling me that even though he was gone, he would always be with me.

Then, a year after his death, I realized how far I'd come. One day I sat outside reading words God had given me to write. As I read the words on the page, memories flooded back. But this time they did not drown me. They did not cut like a sharp knife. Instead they enveloped me, and with tears running down my face

I embraced each and every one of those memories. Part of me was sad because there will not be any new memories with Dave, but there is a greater part of me that is happy that I have all those memories forever, and that my husband is at home in Heaven with God.

*I can do all things through Christ who strengthens me.*

*Philippians 4:13*

# CHAPTER 11

# MAKE EVERY DAY A TUESDAY

*make every day special*

*Surely your goodness and love will follow me
all the days of my life, and I will
dwell in the house of the Lord forever.*

*Psalm 23:6*

On Tuesday February 11, 2014, three days before Valentine's Day, I was standing in the kitchen washing dishes. My husband approached me from behind and gave me the following directions.

1. *Turn around*
2. *Close your eyes*
3. *Put your hands out*

I did those things, but truthfully I was a little annoyed. I thought, *I'm washing dishes. Can't it wait?* What happened next surprised me. My husband put something in my hands (I still had my eyes closed at this point and wasn't sure what it was) and told me to open my eyes. When I looked I saw a beautiful heart-shaped necklace. Both of our names were engraved on the heart, and each one of our birthstones was inside the heart. I looked at my husband and with love told him thank you. Then I joked and said, "You couldn't wait until Friday, could you?" Dave looked at me and smiled, and told me the necklace was not for Valentine's Day. It was just a gift because he loved me. Because it was Tuesday.

I wear that necklace everyday. It means more to me than the biggest diamond ring in the world. I wouldn't trade it for a million trillion dollars. Dave had given me that necklace out of love, just because it was Tuesday. Everyone should try and make every day a Tuesday.

Grief is a daily struggle. Some days are easier than others. So many things I have shared have been struggles. But that is not all that I have experienced on this journey that God has chosen for me. During these times I have grown closer to my youngest daughter Kristen. When she moved back home from Nashville we shared a twelve-hour car ride. Being in an enclosed space for so long is bound to spark some conversation. And it did. We have also experienced several road trips to Illinois. We visited the pumpkin patch we used to frequent when she and her sister were younger. We ate at our favorite restaurants over and over. We went to plays, movies, and concerts. Many evenings we sat home, watched Disney movies, and ate popcorn. We ordered and shared numerous pizzas. I loved every minute of those experiences.

I have developed a closer bond with my colleagues and officemates that can never be broken. They know more about me than I ever thought I would share. They have seen me at my best and at my worst, and they still love me.

I have new friendships, and friendships that were already in existence have been strengthened.

I have a deepened respect, caring, and concern for those people I know who have had loved ones go to Heaven. I get it now. I will never again shy away from going to a visitation or funeral. My feelings don't matter at that moment. It is too important.

I have a different relationship with God. Stronger. God has shown me that even though different can be scary, different is okay.

It's part of his plan. Every day I try to remember to trust God, and I try to remember to follow God. It's tough. But I try. I want to make every day a Tuesday. Below are some of the more positive things I recorded in my journal that have happened on the Tuesdays since my husband's death.

*Tuesday, July 29, 2014: I texted Brandon and thanked him for presenting the flag to me.*

Since Dave had been a member of the Air Force, he received full military honors at his funeral. Brandon also had been in the military and had received permission to present the flag to me. This was a surprise to me, but the memory of Brandon standing in front of me and handing me the flag is with me forever. It was one of the most meaningful parts of Dave's funeral, and I will treasure it forever.

*Tuesday, August 19, 2014: Kristen sent me a text at 12:30 AM to wish me a Happy Birthday.*

To receive a Happy Birthday text from my daughter meant a lot to me. It made me feel so special.

*Tuesday, September 2, 2014: I went to all the places I had planned, talked to all the people I needed to talk to.*

The fact that I finished everything that I had planned was a huge accomplishment. Celebration-worthy. It hasn't always been like that, but that day it was.

*Tuesday, September 16, 2014: I'm still tired but I went to work.*

Some days I just wasn't able to make it to work-whether it was September or April. So when I did make it to work I celebrated in my own way—even if it was done in between yawns.

*Tuesday, September 23, 2014: I'm excited! I'm taking the afternoon off because the decorator is coming. Can't wait to hear her ideas.*

Even though redecorating was stressful, in the end everything turned out very nice.

*Tuesday, October 21, 2014: I shared the music video with the group last night.*

On Father's Day 2014, Kristen sent Dave a very special gift: a link to a new music video that had just been released. We watched it together that day and we both cried. That music video was so meaningful that Kristen chose to show that video at Dave's funeral, and when people visited our house, I often took the opportunity to share that video with them. After I started to attend a grief support group at my church, I knew that they needed to see that music video. Since then others have shared the same music video with important people in their lives.

*Tuesday, November 11, 2014: I stayed at work.*

It sounds like a small thing but it really wasn't. That day had been particularly difficult, but I made the choice to stay at work and not go home.

*Tuesday, February 10, 2015: God has lifted off a layer of the blindfold . . .*

That was a great day when the blindfold started to be removed. I didn't feel like I was in the dark anymore. But with every rainbow there must be some rain. I also realized that there were things that I had been neglecting. And I needed to face those things and deal with them.

*Tuesday, February 17, 2015: I might go to Kohl's to get pillows for the couch.*

This is a positive event for several reasons. First, I was able to go to the store and make a decision about what I wanted to buy. But more importantly, they are really soft pillows! Sometimes it's the little things that make the biggest difference.

*Tuesday, February 24, 2015: Sometimes I think that I'm too tired to do this, or I can't do this. Then I am reminded that God gives me strength and he will never give me more than I can handle.*

Many times I felt like I just couldn't handle things anymore. But each time God reminded me he was in control, giving me all the strength that I needed. I am so blessed.

*Tuesday, March 24, 2015: This trip is so different. I am having a good time. I also know there are people praying and God is guiding me through this trip.*

Going on vacation held its own set of anxieties. I know people were praying and God was working the entire time that we were gone. I really did have a good time.

*Tuesday, March 31, 2015: I trust you Jesus.*

It was always a good day when I could honestly say that I trusted Jesus. There were also many days that I said, "I trust you Jesus" with a little less conviction. But either way I know he heard me.

*Tuesday, April 21, 2015: Dave was in my dreams last night. He was more real, more 3-D. I remembered the Winter Trolley ride and sitting at the English Inn restaurant eating lunch. We had a great time that day. I remember saying something to Dave in my dream. I'm not sure what I said. I know I wanted him to do something.*

I was excited to see Dave in my dreams. I wish I could have remembered what I asked him to do. Whatever it was, I am sure that if he was able to, he would do what I asked. I hope I have that dream again and again.

*Tuesday, April 28, 2015: God is wonderful. He provides for my every need. Sometimes I want more but I know I have what God wants me to have.*

It is human nature to want more. But when you focus on God and are willing to accept that he will give you what you need, (but not always what you want) He will do great things. Trust God and believe that he knows what is best for you.

*Tuesday, May 5, 2015: I got a text yesterday from Brandon. It said, "I thought of the amazing Dave today."*

Something as small as a text like the one Brandon sent me could make my day. I'm sure that message was the best part of my Tuesday. It reminded me again that I was not the only person in the world that thought that Dave was amazing.

*Tuesday, May 19, 2015: I'm good. I mean it . . . That doesn't mean no tears. I think it means less overwhelming feeling, less anxiety, more confidence, more faith and trust in God.*

I meant it when I said I'm good. I will never get over the loss of my husband. But God was showing me how to travel through life without him.

*Tuesday, May 26, 2015: I did it right away without waiting. And I even prayed about it.*

I have developed the bad habit of procrastinating. But on this day I was able to face each one of the tasks on my to-do list without hesitation. That is certainly celebration-worthy.

*Tuesday, June 16, 2015: I do really enjoy being able to stop and relax though.*

Summer was here, and with it came the luxury of being able to sit back and relax and enjoy the beautiful day that God had made. I loved that any day of the week.

*Tuesday, June 23, 2015: It's a beautiful sunny day and I am sitting outside in the shade. With ice on my leg because it itches so badly. I feel like I should be doing something. But then, maybe just sitting here relaxing is doing something. Because I can sit here and enjoy God's beauty. Not a cloud in the sky. A gentle breeze.*

I had gotten an allergic reaction from something, resulting in a very itchy rash on my leg. Sometimes God used things like this to remind me to slow down. So on that Tuesday, instead of complaining about the discomfort that I experienced, I sat and marveled at the beauty of all that God has made.

*Tuesday, June 30, 2015: I got to sleep right away last night!*

My husband used to be able to fall asleep instantly. His head would touch the pillow and he would be in dreamland. I have never been able to do that. So when sleep came quickly, it was always exciting.

*Tuesday July 7, 2015: I went to see a movie today. But this time I thought it over and over before I finally decided to go. I watched the trailers to see if it was something I was ready to see. I still cried, but this time I was prepared for it and it didn't take me by surprise.*

In the past I had gone to movies and not really considered the content (such as having a military funeral). While excellent movies, some of them took me by surprise. This time I was able to think clearly enough to consider all of the possible 'triggers' that it might have. This preparation made all the difference when it came to the sad part of the movie. I knew it was there and I knew I might cry so I was ok with the emotions. Knowing what to expect made all the difference in the world to me.

*Tuesday, July 21, 2015: I bought a new pillow. I've been sleeping a little longer. Don't know if it's just a happy coincidence, but I'm keeping that pillow.*

I went to the store and bought a contoured memory foam pillow. The kind that are supposed to be good for your neck. The kind that I always thought would be uncomfortable. As I put my head on the pillow that evening my first thought was that I liked the pillow. The first few nights using that pillow I didn't wake up as often. It hasn't always been like that, but I am definitely keeping that pillow.

July 24, 2015, was not a Tuesday. But good things happened on that day. Although I was sad and missed my husband, God reminded me that Dave was in Heaven having a really good time. God reminded me that my best friend no longer had pain. God reminded me that his way is best.

*You are my God, and I will give you thanks; you are my God and I will exalt you.*

*Psalm 118:28*

# CHAPTER 12

# LA LA LA LAMBEAU!

*rebuild your life and keep
the good stuff*

*This is the day that the Lord has made; Let us rejoice
and be glad in it.*

*Psalm118:24*

When a loved one dies, things change. When Dave died, it affected every aspect of my life. Something that I learned is that it is necessary to look at each piece of my leftover life and make a decision. Did I want to keep that, or did I want to replace it with something different? And what new things did I want to add to my life? This has been a very difficult task that seems to never end.

Shortly after Dave died a friend asked me why. Why did Dave die? Why did this have to happen to such a good guy? I answered with the only words that I could think of at the time: God had a plan. Shortly after that, in an effort to help him understand what I meant by this, I made a list that I called "pieces of the puzzle." In essence, I was saying that God has a reason for everything that happens. It is only in hindsight that we may be able to see why some things occurred. Here are those puzzle pieces that I wrote in August 2014:

*My job requires me to travel all over the city. Driving is not my favorite pastime, and I am not very good at directions. Taking this job has allowed me to get to know the streets better, which is especially helpful now that my best friend and personal GPS is no longer by my side.*

*We spent time together as a family in Denver during the summer of 2013. We built irreplaceable memories and have professional quality photographs that will be with us forever.*

*Kristen moved to Nashville in January 2014. Because of this the relationship between Dave and Kristen was strengthened, and we were able to spend time together as a family just a few weeks before Dave died.*

*After years of procrastinating, we completed our will. This one step meant that there were no legal issues.*

*I received an iPad through work. This allowed me to stay connected with people on Facebook without having to go downstairs and use the computer.*

*Dave slept downstairs in a comfy chair for a few months before he died (this was helpful for his back). I didn't have to all of a sudden get used to sleeping by myself.*

*I had surgery on my foot in June 2014. It required me to slow down and stop—even when I didn't want to.*

*Dave and I went to my nephew's graduation party the day after my surgery. Everyone was able to see him one last time—even my niece from California who doesn't get home very often.*

*My summer job ended abruptly. While I was worried initially, it allowed me the luxury of not having to decide if or when I would return to work that summer.*

*Brandon took Dave to the Emergency room. I didn't have to face that difficult situation of seeing my husband in pain and having difficulty breathing. By the time I got to the hospital, he was breathing more easily. In fact, all that week I never saw him in pain. I can remember the good times.*

*Dave was in the hospital all week. We spent all of our time together, and I have many happy memories of that week.*

*Dave sent long meaningful texts to both of the girls the morning he died. They will have these forever.*

*Timing for everything was perfect. I was not in the room initially when he became "woozy." The doctor told me on the phone that he was "out of the woods," and I was able to safely drive to the hospital. The doctor was in the room at exactly the right time. People were there for me exactly when I needed it as I made phone calls.*

*Kristen's flight was delayed. The girls ended up on the same flight from Minneapolis and sat next to each other, which was completely unplanned. They were able to support each other.*

I have peace because I know this is part of God's plan. It doesn't mean I'm not sad sometimes. It doesn't mean I don't have tears. It doesn't mean I don't think about him all the time. It means that I believe.

Throughout our married life, Dave and I had talked several times about what we wanted to happen when our lives ended. While we never had anything written on paper, I knew what his wishes were. There was one special song that he wanted to have played at his funeral to encourage other people to keep marching forward. The thing that he was most adamant about was that he never wanted his funeral to be a sad occasion. He wanted people to be happy that he was in Heaven. He wanted it to be a party. As I spoke at his funeral, I shared his feelings. But it was Stacey that best conveyed this message. On the morning of his funeral she told me that she had everything written down, but she made a few changes. As she stood in front of the church that morning and talked about her dad, she ended her speech with these important words.

> *My dad is awesome. I know there is one more thing that my dad would want me to say. "Sprinkler guy, you're at Lambeau Field. La la la Lambeau!"*

I know her dad was smiling as he heard those words. As she walked toward me, I smiled, gave her a hug, and said, "Thank you." That was one of the best gifts she could have ever given me. "La la la Lambeau!" is something I will keep forever, just like the music video that Kristen had sent to Dave on Father's Day. I also want to keep the Packers tradition, visits to the Pumpkin Patch, and going to plays. I want to treasure all of my photographs and memories. It took me several months to get to the point where I was feeling like I was rebuilding my life. I think first my heart had to accept the change that had occurred in my life before I could move on to that step. There are still many things that I am unsure of, but I do know that whatever happens in my new life without my husband, I want it to be approved by God. I want it to be part of his plan.

## New Shoes

I don't buy new shoes very often. Part of the reason is that after I have worn a pair of shoes for a while, they fit my feet perfectly and become very comfy. I want to wear them every day. Though I hate to compare my marriage to an old pair of shoes, after almost twenty-nine years of being married we knew each other very well.

We were safe and comfortable with each other. When my husband died, things changed. God taught me I needed to accept my new life without my husband. This lesson was not learned overnight, and it took a lot of trust and faith. I still think about the way things used to be, but I know that part of my life is in the past. I have a new life to build and live.

Part of building my new life involved participating in some of the same things as my past. Going to Disney was one of those things. Kristen and I went to Disney, but it was different than when we had gone as a family. Besides the fact that someone important was missing, the experience was different. But I learned that I could still have fun if things were different.

Another part of rebuilding my life has been accepting that things are different. So many times I have wanted to hold on to the way things were. That is just not a good idea. Remembering and treasuring memories is an important part of grief. That is something that you should never stop doing. But letting go is a necessary step in the grief process. Letting go does not mean you love someone any less. In fact, I think just the opposite. For me, it means that I love Dave so much that I will let him go and move forward with my life. I know that Dave would want me to do that.

When Dave and I got married, building our life was relatively easy. When it came to making decisions, we were able to discuss things together. Unfortunately, sometimes we forgot to include God in our conversations. When my husband died, things changed. I needed to rebuild my life, but this time without my best friend by my side. I had to learn to rely on God more and more. For both the big things and the little things.

God never asks us to do something without giving us the strength that we need to accomplish the task. When God took Dave to Heaven, I knew right away he had a plan. What I didn't understand was what that would mean for my life. Through faith, prayer, and tears I am slowly learning that I don't have to understand why. I just need to believe God. He will take care of the rest, and he is helping me to rebuild my life. I still miss Dave. He will forever be my always. God is now teaching me to live my life without my husband and best friend by my side.

## Keep On Keeping On

I usually talked to my mom on the telephone once a week. I was surprised when she asked me about doing something different, and I'm not exactly sure why she asked. But in all honesty I had already had that talk with God. Soon after my husband died I told God I would be willing to do whatever he wanted me to do. Over time God made it clear he wanted me to remain teaching for the rest of the school year. Even so, there were times that work was overwhelming. There were times that even though I knew that I could do the job, I didn't know what it would look like. But I wanted to make sure that I was following the path God set before me so that I could rebuild my life according to his will. I plan on returning to teaching next school year and the next. Unless God reveals to me a different plan. I am willing to follow wherever he leads me.

*Show me your ways, LORD, teach me your paths.*

*Psalm 25:4*

As I have written, I am not good at directions. Not at all. I like to know from the beginning what the route is going to be, where I am going to turn and where I will end up. Rebuilding my life has challenged me in all of these areas. God has not sent me a list of directions, and he has not told me what the end destination will be. I have had to have faith and trust that God will tell me where and when I need to turn. I know that if I don't listen the first time, God will recalculate the directions and do whatever is necessary to help me hear the next time.

The spring after Dave died, I wrote this in my journal: *Then as I was driving I realized that I am rebuilding my life. With every step I take, I am rebuilding my life. I want to make sure God is always the biggest part of my life.*

It was on this day that I realized that everything I did was part of rebuilding my life. Every time I prayed, I was confirming that I wanted God to be first in my life. Every time I connected with a friend, I was confirming that relationships were an important part of my life. Every time I took a step, I was confirming that I wanted to continue on the path that God set before me. These were all conscious decisions that I made; ones that I knew were necessary. Even though I didn't have the full plan, God was showing me the next step to take.

Part of grieving is accepting that someone you love has died, and accepting and building your new life. Along this grief path I have learned many things. One of those things is that it is not only okay, but it is necessary to move forward with your life. It is okay to like and to feel happy about different aspects of your new life. That does not mean there will not be emotions attached to those feelings. Guilt is a normal part of grief. I was able to laugh and smile without feeling bad, but I still wondered if it was okay to enjoy things. I knew the answer was yes. But for some reason writing the words always helped me to accept these feelings.

Writing helps put the puzzle pieces in place. And after Dave died, I was faced with the job of putting a puzzle back together with pieces that don't fit. I needed to let God fit the pieces together.

One of the things that was helpful as I began rebuilding my life was realizing that it was a difficult task. A task that never ends. A task that can be best approached with God.

As I worked to rebuild my life, there was always one thing that I knew that I wanted. I knew that I wanted God to be at the front of my life. I wanted to do whatever God had planned for me. I knew that there was no right or wrong when it came to grief, but

I still had doubts as to whether I was "doing grief right." So each and every day I prayed and asked God to show me what to do next.

Part of rebuilding my life was listening to and following God. When God told me to write a book, I said, "Okay."

I didn't realize just how much faith and courage would be involved in such an endeavor. Right away I knew that I would need to and wanted to speak to people and ask their permission to use their names in the book. God provided the courage I needed to reach out to people. I was always prepared in case someone told me no. For some reason, I was always surprised at the positive reaction I received. Looking back, I'm not sure why I ever doubted this. After all, I knew that this was God's idea.

In fact, working on the book helped me recognize one of the best things to happen as I worked to rebuild my life: I have become more aware of all the blessings in my life. Every day I count my blessings.

Through this process, I've felt God working in my life. The more time I spent with God, the closer I became to him.

*The LORD is near to all who call upon him, to all who call upon him in truth.*

*Psalm 145:18*

## Together

Dave and I did things together. And we missed each other when we were apart. I'm not saying we acted like we hadn't seen each other for years when we were reunited after a long day at work. Our love for each other was there, and we both knew it. Our love for each other got us through some difficult storms. Getting used to doing things without my husband has been difficult, but I have learned that I can still have fun. It just feels different.

For instance, one day Kristen asked me to go with her to a bookstore. This particular bookstore was located in Rockford,

Illinois. When Dave was alive, the thought of hopping in a car in the middle of the week to drive 190 miles to go to a bookstore was not a thought that he ever entertained (although he would drive even farther to play golf). But when Kristen asked me that day to go, I could not for the life of me think of a reason not to go. One year ago I would not have considered the idea, but that day I agreed. In this life things change, and we need to be willing to change also.

Sometimes change means being willing to go it alone. I had been invited to a Fourth-of-July cookout at my sister-in-law's house. Kristen was working that day so I went by myself. It wasn't that I didn't want to go there, because I did. It wasn't that I didn't want to see all of Dave's relatives, because I did. I had a great time. It wasn't that I needed someone to go with me. It's just that I wished that my husband were still there and that he could have joined me for the fun that day. But that part of my life has changed, and I have had to learn to go places by myself. Because that's what you have to do when someone you love has died.

I've found you also have to learn to let go.

Yes, part of grief is going through closets and getting rid of things. But it doesn't mean everything. This job has to be done, but for me it has been done little by little. As I am ready I pull things off of a shelf or out of a closet and make a decision about it. If I'm not sure, or if it causes anxiety, I keep it. I can always go back to it another time. Maybe then I will be ready for that memory.

As I've moved forward in my new life, I have had to face many things. Many times people seemed unsure as to whether or not they should talk about Dave. Often they thought it would "remind me" that he had died. So I wanted to help people learn how to find out if or when it was okay to talk about a loved one that had died. The answer I came to was simple. Just ask. I'm okay with people asking if it's okay to talk about my husband. My answer will always be yes. However, when you ask this question, it is important to listen to the answer. But more important than the words that they might say are the actions that they demonstrate. Because you can say a lot without ever speaking any words. If you want to know something, just ask. Then watch and listen.

## Safe in the Storms

The summer after my husband died I drove to Chicago and dropped Kristen off for a concert. I then ventured back onto the highway and headed to my sister's house, about forty miles away. By the time I had started on this trip, the rain had begun and soon turned into a raging storm. Amid the downpour my gas gauge read empty, and I had to stop for gas. I was quickly soaked. But I didn't drown. Throughout the long trip, I had times of darkness and times I didn't know where I was going. It reminded me of the past year when those same emotions surfaced. I often had felt lost and scared, but I knew that God would always guide me to where he wanted me to be. God kept me safe.

A year after my husband died, I wrote him this letter:

*So, Dave, it's been an entire year without you. I hope I did okay. I hope that you have been watching (can you do that?) and seeing everything. The girls have been amazing. I can't believe how strong they are. You have a new nephew—he's almost a year old now. I wish you could have been here to meet him. As for me, I'm doing okay. I miss you more than you can imagine. Things just aren't the same without you, but I'm trying to pick up the pieces and let God put them back together. But I would really love a hug from you. Someday.*

*I love you Dave*
*You will forever be my always*

As I wrote this, I didn't think. I just wrote what was in my heart. So much has happened in the year since my husband died.

I do wonder if people in Heaven have a window to see their loved ones. I like to think that they can. As for me, I *am* doing okay. I am still sad at times, and I still miss my husband more than I could have ever imagined possible. But I also know that God has a plan, one that is much better than I could have ever dreamed of. I will move forward in my life, but I will always remember and treasure the memories of the years that I had with my husband. And I will look forward to seeing him again in Heaven someday, when I will finally receive the best hug in the world. Someday.

*The Lord is my shepherd, I shall not want.*

*Psalm 23:1*

# THE BASICS (REVISITED)

*the foundational basis in my life has not changed—it has only become stronger*

*For no one can lay any foundation other than the one already laid, which is Jesus Christ.*

*1 Corinthians 3:11*

* I love my husband. He will forever be my always.
* I have never for a second doubted that Dave's death was God's will.
* I love my husband. I always have and I always will.
* Grief is the most difficult, confusing, exhausting thing that I have ever experienced.
* I love my husband. There were a million little things about him that made our relationship special.
* I could never have gone through this without God.
* I love my husband. And I know he loved me more than anything in the world.
* I don't like roller coasters.
* I love my husband. He didn't like roller coasters either.
* Life is like a puzzle.

* I love my husband. That part, the best part of my life, is now dancing in Heaven.
* God is in control. He always has been and always will.
* I love my husband. I will never forget that I was able to spend so many years with my first true love.
* Even when I don't see or feel him, God is always there. He is with me through the darkest part of the night and the brightest part of the day.

# AFTERWORD

My journey through grief is far from over. However, it is at this point that this part of the story will stop. Along the way I have learned some very important things.

*About ups and downs*: God is in control of all the twists, turns, and drops in my life. He is also in control of all the parts that feel calm and manageable. I have learned to turn to God at all times and be willing to listen to what he has to say. God is patient, and he will continue speaking and telling you things until you finally listen and hear.

*About socks*: Sometimes the hardest decisions to make are the ones that seem of least importance. But God first gives us an opportunity to make small decisions to prepare us for the bigger decisions. Socks. They really are important.

*About stamina*: There are times in our lives we feel we just can't go on any further. We feel like we just can't take another step without falling. When that happens, God is telling us to rest and to lean on him. We don't have to do everything in our life by ourselves. God is telling us to reach out to others and to share each other's heartaches.

*About health*: Overall physical health in our lives is something that is often taken for granted or overlooked. We know that when illness occurs, we can always go to a doctor and get some antibiotics to help heal whatever we are afflicted with at the time. Along this journey, my physical health has been challenged, and each time I sought assistance to help heal whatever was plaguing me at the time. Unfortunately, spiritual health is also something that is ignored. At times we assume that as long as we believe Jesus died on the cross for us then we can live our lives doing whatever we want. Nothing could be further from the truth. God wants us to spend time with him daily. He delights in it.

*About changes and differences*: In this life, things change. Even when we like something and enjoy it there is always the potential for things to become different. Different is not bad. While we may not understand now, God has a reason for changing things. There is a purpose to what we may see as chaos and tragedy. We may never know the reason for why things happen, but we do need to trust and believe that God has everything under control and that his ideas are better than anything we could have ever imagined. Different can be scary. Different can be sad. But different is okay.

*About people*: Most people do not know what to say or do when someone dies. They go through the rituals of attending the final services, sending a card, and offering their condolences. But unless you have had a similar experience, no one really knows what to do or say. I learned that there were people around me that were willing to wait as I struggled to breathe, people who were willing to listen as I searched for the right words to express myself, and people who prayed for me. During the past year, I have also learned that there were times I needed to be the one to let people know that it was okay to talk about my husband. There were times that I had to let things go, and accept the fact that unless someone had walked along this difficult journey, there was no way possible they could come close to understanding what I was feeling. I learned to thank God for each and every person along this journey, because God had a reason for putting each one of those people in my life at that time.

*About faith*: Sometimes faith really does mean just tying your shoes. It was difficult but I came to accept this, and there were times that when someone would ask me how I was doing I would respond by telling them, "My shoes are tied. I'm good." I learned that faith means believing that God is there with me, even when I can't see or feel him. I also learned that even when I have faith and believe that everything will work out, tears may flow. I came to understand my tears were not a sign of weakness, but a sign that I loved someone very deeply. Even Jesus wept.

*About choices*: There are good choices and not-so-good choices. But each choice has a consequence. I learned that before I made a choice, I needed to consider several things. First of all, would my choice cause harm to anyone—either physical, emotional, or spiritual? Is this something that I want to do? But most importantly of all: is this what God wants me to do? I have spent countless hours in prayer asking God for guidance about my life. He has not given me a roadmap of my life for the next few years. Instead he is directing me on the path I should travel. I have learned to travel step by step with my eyes and ears tuned to God. But I also know that if I step off the path he has prepared for me he will gently guide me back to where I need to be.

*About confidence*: After my husband died, my confidence in earthly things was shattered. However, my confidence and belief in God remained strong. I knew God had a purpose for taking my husband to Heaven on that day. In fact, there were days that the only thing that I was sure of was that his death was part of God's plan. Sometimes that was the only thing that made sense. God used my confidence in him to show me that I could live my life without my best friend. God is using that confidence in him to remind me that even though there are times I am sad, I will see my husband again in Heaven someday.

*About Tuesdays:* On Tuesday February 11, 2014, my husband gave me a heart-shaped necklace because he loved me. Just because it was Tuesday. At the time I didn't understand the significance, but I have since learned that it is important to make every day special. We celebrate special days like Christmas and Thanksgiving, but we tend to trudge through the non-holidays and not pay as much attention to them. We should try and make each day special. We should remember to make each day a Tuesday.

*About Lambeau*: Rebuilding your life is a necessary part of grief. Someone you love is no longer there, and you need to learn how to move forward without that person. For me it was important to keep busy. I always needed to have a project to focus on. Making Christmas ornaments, redecorating the house, creating videos, and designing a scrapbook were just a few of my projects. I went to work, but often my heart just wasn't there. I went out with friends and visited family but it was never the same. It wasn't until my heart truly accepted that my husband had died that I was able to begin rebuilding my life. Little by little, I began to see that God was showing me how to start putting the pieces of my shattered life back together. As this happened, I could see differences in what my life used to look like and what it was becoming. I realized that there were some things that really weren't that important to me after all, and I was able to let go of those things. God has allowed me to keep the good things, such as my memories of my life with Dave. He is also allowing me to build new memories with my daughters and the many friends and family that have shared this journey with me. I will never forget the time that I was able to spend with Dave, and I will cherish each and every memory. He will forever be my always.

Thank you for joining me as I shared these words God inspired me to write (I could never have written anything like this by myself). Sometime during your lifetime you may experience the death of someone you love. If this happens know that it is part of God's plan, and he will always be right there with you. He is navigating that roller coaster, and he will never let you fall.

*"For I know the plans I have for you," declares the Lord,*
*"plans to prosper you and not to harm you,*
*plans to give you hope and a future."*

*Jeremiah 29:11*

On Tuesday September 15, 2015, I held on tightly as the roller coaster made a horrendous drop and began to spin violently. Thirteen months and twenty-two days after my husband died, my nephew Jack went home to Heaven. He was five years old. My journey had suddenly taken on a new intensity. Though I felt darkness for a time, I also saw light. God was still there. He did not let me fall.

I love you, Jack, and always will. Say hi to your Uncle Dave for me and give him a big hug. You and Uncle Dave will never be forgotten.

Connect with the Author:
cmbarnum1@gmail.com
www.Facebook.com/WhytheJourneyMatters
Twitter: @CarolMBarnum